SHIRE GARDEN HISTORY

A Glossary of Garden History

Michael Symes

D1308182

Published in 2000 by Shire Publications, Cromwell House, Church Street, Princes Risborough, Buckinghamshire HP27 9AA, UK. Website: www.shirebooks.co.uk
Copyright © 1993 and 2000 by Michael Symes. First published 1993. Second edition 2000. Number 6 in the Shire Garden History series. ISBN 0 7478 0439 7.

Printed in Great Britain by CIT Printing Services Ltd, Press Buildings, Merlins Bridge, Haverfordwest, Pembrokeshire SA61 1XF.

British Library Cataloguing in Publication Data: Symes, Michael. Glossary of Garden History. – (Shire Garden History Series; No. 6) I. Title II. Series 712.09. ISBN 0-7478-0439-7.

(Cover photograph) *The cascade at West Wycombe Park, Buckinghamshire.*

(Title page) *An engraving of David Garrick's garden at Hampton, Middlesex (1779).*

ACKNOWLEDGEMENTS

Photographs are acknowledged as follows: Jacqueline Fearn, page 30; French National Tourist Office, page 51; Dorothy Anne Robinson, page 46 (below); Michael Symes, pages 11, 13 (top right and below), 17 (top and centre), 23, 31 (below), 32 (top), 38 (left), 41 (below left), 43 (below), 49, 56 (below left and right), 57 (centre), 59, 60 (top), 62, 64 (below), 74 (left), 75, 81 (left), 82 (below), 86 (below right), 91 (left), 92, 97 (left), 101, 107, 113, 117 (top right), 124, 125 (left and centre), 127 (below), 131 and 133 (top left). The remainder, including the cover photograph, are by Cadbury Lamb.

Contents

Introduction 5

Glossary 9

Appendix: Some major British garden designers 136

Further reading 141

Index of people and places 142

The Garden History Society 144

Guns and cannon: Milton Lodge, Somerset.

Arch: Hadrian's Arch, Shugborough, Staffordshire.

Introduction

Garden history as a recognisable subject is a comparatively recent phenomenon. From the earliest times there has been interest in creating gardens and writing about them, and there have been various histories of gardening, but as an identifiable academic area it has developed only since the Second World War. The pioneers, who treated gardens as objects for serious aesthetic and archival investigation, were Frank Clark and Christopher Hussey, whose 'milestone' books *The English Landscape Garden* and *English Gardens and Landscapes 1700-1750* came out in 1948 and 1967 respectively. During this time too Dorothy Stroud explored the work of 'Capability' Brown and Humphry Repton in a scholarly way, to be followed by Kenneth Woodbridge's researches into, and interpretation of, the gardens of Stourhead, Wiltshire.

Another landmark at this period from a British viewpoint was the formation of the Garden History Society in 1965. This was initially an attempt to bring together those who were interested in the proper study of garden history. Since then the Society has gone from strength to strength and now has an important, and still growing, role in garden conservation, while not losing sight of its original purpose.

Interest in garden history has expanded enormously since 1965. Individual gardens have been studied in depth, through archives, archaeology and surveying; individual garden designers and their work have been scrutinised in detail; and, based on original research which is still revealing new data and surprises, there has been an increasing number of surveys of periods of garden history in various countries, of features such as garden buildings or overviews of cultural or other influences.

It is an interdisciplinary subject, related to many others, including architecture, the history of art, horticulture, botany, literature, philosophy, social history and politics. Several of those who are famed for their achievement in other spheres, such as the poet Alexander Pope (1688-1744), have found gardening and garden design to be of equal importance to their major activity.

Sometimes the links with other subjects are inextricable, so that an owner's or designer's garden design is the expression of a creativity that fuses or synthesises other interests. For example, in the case of Charles Hamilton at Painshill, Surrey (mid eighteenth century), or R. S. Holford at Westonbirt, Gloucestershire (nineteenth century), a passion for planting and a love of collecting new species combine with an artist's eye for design and layout.

Archival research has, since 1980, been supplemented by increasingly sophisticated fieldwork in the form of surveys and garden archaeology. Tree surveys, pollen analysis, soil analysis and archaeological techniques have all been used to provide a clearer picture of a garden's past.

Historic gardens in Britain have not enjoyed as full protection as buildings, but grants are available for conservation and restoration and gardens are listed in a National Register compiled under the auspices of English Heritage. As with buildings, gardens are listed in categories that reflect their importance. The Garden History Society is a statutory consultee in cases of development plans that might affect an historic park or garden.

In addition to English Heritage as the official overseer of historic gardens, there is much interest and work at local level. Gardens of all kinds from past to modern are investigated and monitored by individual county gardens trusts, which are linked by the Association of Gardens Trusts. Working in tandem with English Heritage, the county trusts can defend important gardens against building developments or other threats, as well as educating the local populace in the knowledge and understanding of gardens in the area. In the case of some particular gardens, individual trusts have been established.

There are specialist groups such as the Georgian Group, the Victorian Society and the Twentieth-Century Society which have a particular interest in gardens of their respective periods, while the National Council for the Conservation of Plants and Gardens is concerned with the recording, documentation and conservation of rare garden plants (whether ancient or modern).

In the field of education, there are many courses at various levels which deal with all aspects of the subject from academic to practical and professional. Some courses are concerned with garden history as such while others are more geared to conservation and management.

The glossary explains the major terms likely to be encountered when reading garden history or visiting historic gardens. Rare or out-of-the-way terms are not included, since there must be limits to the number of words that can be covered. It is *not* a dictionary of gardening, of botany or of architecture, for which there is provision elsewhere. A few basic terms from these areas, however, are included: thus, in architecture the orders are listed, because references to Doric, Ionic and so on occur so frequently, but not individual parts of a building as separate entries (e.g. cornice, architrave), except for finial, which is often a garden ornament in its own right. Similarly, techniques of gardening are not included except where the result, e.g. espalier, has some impact on the appearance of a garden or features significantly in the history of garden design.

Characteristics of the work of individual designers may occur under various headings. Although some entries relate to style, I have resisted the temptation to use adjectives derived from designers (Reptonian, Robinsonian) except in the case of Brownian, where the stylistic elements form such an important part of the concept of the English landscape garden and also of the Picturesque controversy (q.v.). Major British designers are listed in the Appendix.

Individual entries range from simple meaning to derivation and usage, with examples cited and illustrated where appropriate. In some cases I have made use of contemporary definitions from works such as Philip Miller's *Gardeners Dictionary*, which went through several editions in the eighteenth century. The emphasis is on Britain, but examples are chosen also from other countries if applicable, particularly France and Italy, which have had such long and strong traditions of garden-making.

Definitions given are within a garden history context and therefore may have wider and sometimes different application elsewhere. In such an undertaking one is heavily indebted to the work of others, and in the bibliography I have listed the works which have provided much useful source material. My grateful thanks go to a number of garden historians who have helped, including Brent Elliott, John Harvey, Paula Henderson and Mark Laird. Other friends who have provided information include Valerie Monaghan and Pat Reynolds. I am particularly indebted to Mavis Batey, Peter Goodchild and Nigel Temple for their advice on the range of entries and comments on the entries themselves. Any gaps or blemishes are entirely my responsibility.

I acknowledge with gratitude the permission of the Oxford University Press to reuse material which I had contributed to *The Oxford Companion to Gardens*.

Alcove: Manderston, Borders.

Ambulatory: Horton Court, Avon.

Glossary

Adonis (classical). Adonis was regarded in mythology as the author and nourisher of all seeds. Pliny originated the idea of Adonis having a garden, and small 'gardens of Adonis' in earthen pots were placed before the temples of Adonis at the annual festival in his honour. Plants such as lettuce were sown in the pots and would quickly wither to symbolise the early death of Adonis.

Aeolian harp. A cross between a lyre and a zither, this instrument was set in gardens or other open spaces for the wind to play the strings.

Alcove. A recess in a garden wall or hedge; later, a covered retreat or bower. It may house sculpture or a seat and is often a larger version of the niche. An alcove is sometimes synonymous with seat.

Alhambra (Arabic). A garden building in Moorish style. The most famous in an English garden was Sir William Chambers's Alhambra at Kew, Surrey (1758), one of a number of exotic or oriental buildings grouped together there.

Allée (French). A straight walk in a garden, lined by trees or hedges. It is of gravel, sand or turf and has some breadth, though not as much as an avenue. It often creates a vista, with an object of interest (building, etc) at the far end.

Alley. A walk in a garden or shrubbery; or a long narrow area for games such as bowls or ninepins. As the former it is equivalent to the allée.

Allotment. A piece of land let out under municipal or other public arrangement to individuals for growing vegetables, etc ; originally part of a field allotted to a cottager for private cultivation.

Alpine garden. A garden which features rocks and rock-loving plants that require little water. The rock may either occur naturally or be brought in. Alpine plants do not come exclusively from the Alps but from many mountainous regions.

Alpine house (nineteenth century onwards). Garden house with plenty of ventilation and no heating for the display and cultivation of Alpine species.

Ambulatory (medieval). Covered cloister-type walk detached from the house, as at Horton Court, Avon.

American garden. A garden planted with species obtained from, or native to, North America. The idea evolved during the eighteenth century, when, through the Bartrams in Pennsylvania and Peter Collinson in London, many trees and shrubs were made available to owners and designers in England. Humphry Repton designed American gardens for a number of sites including Ashridge, Hertfordshire, and Woburn Abbey, Bedfordshire, while William Beckford created an enormous American plantation at Fonthill, Wiltshire. Many conifers were grown, together with rhododendrons, magnolias, azaleas, tulip trees and liquidambars. By the 1840s the term was extended to refer to an area in which acid-loving plants from many parts of the world were grown.

Amphitheatre. (1) A garden feature of turf cut into ramps and stepped terraces, straight or curving. It may resemble the shape of a classical amphitheatre but does not have to do so. The late seventeenth-century French designer Dezallier d'Argenville illustrated and described this sort of feature, which was developed in the early eighteenth century in England by Charles Bridgeman, whose amphitheatres survive at Claremont in Surrey, Cliveden in Buckinghamshire and Rousham, Oxfordshire (vestigial).

(2) A concave bowl-like land form where the trees create a tiered effect by virtue of being planted at different heights, such as at Mount Edgcumbe, Cornwall, or Park Place (near Henley), Berkshire (both eighteenth century).

(3) A scheme where trees and shrubs are planted in a circle on the level but in progressive rows so that the tallest are at the back, again producing a tiered appearance, such as at Painshill, Surrey.

(4) An area for open-air performance, inspired by classical amphitheatres though not necessarily modelled on them in appearance. An example is at the Boboli gardens, Florence, where pageants, masques and theatrical displays took place.

Apiary: Biddick Hall, Tyne and Wear.

Aqueduct: Arkadia, Poland.

Anglo-Chinois. The French term for the English landscape style of garden. When the pictorial English landscape movement reached France from the middle of the eighteenth century, a feeling grew up there that the style owed as much to Chinese irregularity of form as to English ideas. This was fanned by the popularity of the French translations of Sir William Chambers's works on Chinese gardens and designs. The concept was vigorously rebutted by Horace Walpole, among others, who attributed it to jealousy: 'they deny us half the merit or rather originality of the invention, by ascribing the discovery to the Chinese.'

Apiary. Enclosure or area where bees are kept. Biddick Hall, Tyne and Wear, has an apiary with a series of Chinese-style beehives.

Approach. The drive or road leading from an estate entrance to the house. Humphry Repton distinguished between a drive (q.v.), which toured around all the places and views of interest within the park, and an approach, which should lead in a winding but not too tortuous way to the house, affording some views of scenes or objects which could be explored subsequently. At Blaise Castle, Bristol, there are both an approach and a drive. A typical sweeping Repton approach is at Port Eliot, Cornwall.

Aqueduct. A bridge or similar structure carrying water across a valley. There is a large aqueduct in the stupendous garden of water effects at Wilhelmshöhe, Germany, and a small ruined one (c.1790) at Arkadia, Poland, which was intended functionally as a bridge not an aqueduct, with a cascade beneath.

Arable land. Land suitable or used for ploughing and the sowing of crops.

Arboretum. A collection of trees of different sorts. The concept developed from the seventeenth century in Britain. The principal interest is botanical, but arboreta can be laid out artistically with regard to groupings and walks, as at Westonbirt Arboretum, Gloucestershire (from 1829). See also *Pinetum.*

Arbour. A garden shelter or bower, often of curving arch form. See also *Tunnel-arbour* and *Pergola.*

Arcade. A series of arches linked together. William Kent designed a loggia-like arcade, called Praeneste (q.v.), at Rousham, Oxfordshire (1730s), while a Gothic arcade forms part of the late eighteenth-century pictorial park at Arkadia, Poland. An arcade can also be made out of a hedge clipped into arch shapes, tree trunks forming the uprights, as formerly at Hartwell House, Buckinghamshire (c.1740).

Arch. A curved structure, generally surmounting and connecting two uprights. In gardens an arch can be of various materials, such as trellis, stone or brick. Ornamental arches were often used as garden features and eyecatchers, e.g. Hadrian's Arch on a hill at Shugborough, Staffordshire (c.1760), or the Corinthian Arch at Stowe, Buckinghamshire (1765), which is large enough to serve as a dwelling. Painshill, Surrey, has a mausoleum which is in the form of a ruined Roman triumphal arch. See also *Reposoir.*

Archery ground. An area for the practice of archery, as at Bowood, Wiltshire. Cf. *Bowling green* and *Alley* for areas laid out for other pastimes.

Armillary sphere. A sundial consisting of a sphere formed from a number of solid rings, as at the American Museum, Claverton Manor, Bath, Avon.

Artinatural. A term coined by Batty Langley to denote an intermediate style between formal and informal which he also called 'regular irregularity'. In his *Practical Geometry* (1726) and *New Principles of Gardening* (1728) Langley advances the design principle of a basic axial geometry but with serpentine and asymmetrical lines appearing within otherwise orderly compartments. The entire plan may indeed be asymmetrical, with a mixture of straight and wavy lines.

Arts and Crafts (late Victorian and Edwardian). The movement initiated by John Ruskin and William Morris led, in gardening, to the use of traditional crafts and materials for garden structures. In layout and planting, however, there was no single approach to

Arbour: example in yew, Antony, Cornwall.

Armillary sphere: Claverton Manor, Avon.

follow, and gardens could vary from the informal cottage garden to Lutyens's ordered geometry, where the hand of the architect was evident.

Auricula theatre. A shelter open at the front with tiered shelving for the display of auriculas, to protect them from the rain. There were a number in the early nineteenth century, when there was a craze for brightly coloured varieties. A rare survivor is at Calke Abbey, Derbyshire. Other flowers may be displayed according to season (see illustration).

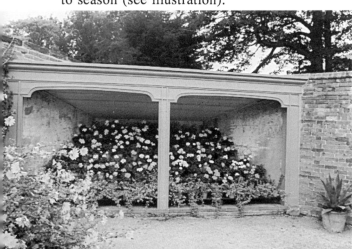

Auricula theatre: Calke Abbey, Derbyshire.

Automata. Italian Renaissance garden owners delighted in mechanical figures, birds and animals which performed according to clockwork or wind or water power, e.g. at the Villa d'Este or Villa Aldobrandini. Sometimes the figures would be constructed to produce giochi d'acqua (q.v.). In France, at St Germain-en-Laye, the water powered various machines to play musical instruments.

Avenue. A tree-lined way or approach, usually long and broad (originally, simply an approach). It can be inside or outside a garden or carry the garden out into and through the park, such as the gigantic avenues at Cirencester Park, Gloucestershire, or Badminton, Avon. As part of formal designs avenues are normally straight. A number of avenues can be found in Hampton Court, Middlesex, and the adjoining Bushy Park.

Aviary. A large cage for housing and displaying birds of various kinds. There have been many very attractive aviaries in gardens, such as the early nineteenth-century Chinese aviary at Dropmore, Buckinghamshire. An elaborate enclosed pheasant aviary of a pavilion shape with smaller wing pavilions is at Waddesdon Manor, Buckinghamshire (1888). An aviary called an eagle's cage is at Dirnanean, Tayside.

Axial. A layout centred on an axis or principal line which usually relates to the house. A formal garden can be structured on a number

Aviary: Waddesdon Manor, Buckinghamshire.

Banqueting house: Studley Royal, North Yorkshire.

of axes which may be parallel to, or at right angles to, one another, or sometimes diagonal. A garden such as Versailles has a main central axis and several subsidiary axes.

Bagnio (Italian = bath house). The Casina at Chiswick, Middlesex, was sometimes so called to indicate one of its functions (it contained a cold bath).

Balustrade. A row of balusters, with a coping rail, forming a parapet, often on a terrace. They are commonly found in Italian or Italianate gardens. 'Baluster' originally denoted the blossom of the pomegranate, which has the same shape.

Banqueting house. A garden room or house away from the main house, for eating and entertainment. In Tudor times at least, the eating was confined to light refreshment (desserts and confectionery) rather than serious feasting but, later, more substantial meals were served. The Banqueting Hall at Mowbray Point, Hackfall, North Yorkshire (c.1750), has a kitchen and servants' hall nearby, while the Banqueting House at Studley Royal, North Yorkshire, originally an orangery (1730), had a kitchen subsequently attached. A memorable Gothic banqueting house at Gibside, Tyne and Wear (1751), has been restored.

Bark hut. See under *Moss hut.*

Baroque (in Britain, late seventeenth/early eighteenth centuries). Formal French-style layout on a grand scale.

Basin. The bowl for the water in a fountain; an artificial pool often fed by fountains or cascades. The term is also applied to large geometrical ponds, e.g. the octagon basin at Wanstead, Essex.

Bastion. In gardens, a projecting bay or corner vantage point. The garden at Grimsthorpe, Lincolnshire, had a walled garden with several corner angles, each comprising an arrowhead bastion. A huge military garden was constructed at Blenheim, Oxfordshire, with a curtain wall and eight round bastions each 50 metres wide. The military associations of the bastion were sometimes specifically evoked: the bays in the terrace walk at Farnborough Hall, Warwickshire (c.1750), look out, appropriately, over the site of Civil War battlefields. A projecting walled bastion can be seen at Goldney, Bristol.

Bath. See *Cold bath.*

Bath house. A structure covering, or beside, a cold bath. Sometimes it would be over a spring, as with the thatched 'Roman' bath house at Painshill, Surrey (c.1790), and elaborate examples such as those at Packwood House, Warwickshire, or Corsham Court, Wiltshire, might have changing rooms and even fires in addition to the bath itself. At Rousham, Oxfordshire, the bath is alfresco and the bath house is adjacent. A wonderful rococo bath house attributed to Thomas Wright at Wrest Park, Bedfordshire, has an antechamber or changing room with a pebble floor lined with sheep's knuckle bones.

Bath house and Bradford Porch: Corsham Court, Wiltshire.

*Bastion:
Goldney,
Bristol, Avon.*

*Bath house:
floor of
pebbles and
sheep's
knuckle bones,
Wrest Park,
Bedfordshire.*

*Bath house:
Raby Castle,
County
Durham.*

Battery. A strip where cannon are sited. Batteries that were actually used have been incorporated into garden scenery for their visual effect and as vantage points for views, as at Mount Edgcumbe, Cornwall. Sham batteries were sometimes made, as at West Wycombe, Buckinghamshire, overlooking the lake, where mock naval battles were fought, and at Clumber Park, Nottinghamshire.

Beautiful. The later eighteenth century was much given to aesthetic categorising – see also *Sublime* and *Picturesque*. The Beautiful, as enunciated by the Herefordshire squires Sir Uvedale Price and Richard Payne Knight, had a smooth, undulating appearance, with no harshness, surprise or broken lines. This is cognate with Hogarth's waving line of beauty in the 1750s, while Edmund Burke's treatise on 'The Sublime and the Beautiful' (1757) included also the elements of gradual variation and delicacy of form. Many mid-century landscape gardens exhibit the concept of smooth beauty, from the Claude-inspired pictorial scenery at Stourhead, Wiltshire, to Brown's serene parks.

Bed. A plot of earth for the raising of flowers, vegetables and shrubs.

Bedding out. The practice of planting flowers (usually annuals) in beds after first growing them in pots in a greenhouse. In this way a display of flowers can be changed two or three times a year in the same beds. Many large public gardens employ this system, e.g. Hampton Court, Middlesex. It dates from the 1830s.

Bee bole. A niche, often with arched top, in a thick garden wall to protect bee-skeps (the predecessors of the modern hive). Sometimes the arches could be decorative. A series of bee boles can be found at Packwood House, Warwickshire, and also at Troy House, Gwent (1611).

Bee house. A house for sheltering bee hives or skeps in rows on shelves or stands. A wooden bee house is preserved at Attingham Park, Shropshire.

Belt (especially eighteenth century). (1) The planting of trees round the perimeter of an estate, with or without a drive. Designs for belts can be found in Stephen Switzer's books, and many of 'Capability' Brown's plans included a belt of trees, good examples being at Petworth, West Sussex, and Wimpole Hall, Cambridgeshire. Since the belt delineates the boundary of the grounds, it runs counter to the approach of William Kent, who opened up the estate to let the country outside seem part of it.
(2) The perimeter drive, from which the visitor could look continually into and across the grounds.

Belvedere (Italian = beautiful to see, hence to give a fine view

Battery: Culzean Castle, Strathclyde.
Belvedere: Alfred's Tower,
Stourhead, Wiltshire.
Bee bole: Packwood House, Warwickshire.

from). (1) In general, a raised structure to provide a commanding or attractive view, as at the Belvedere Palace, Vienna, or the Belvedere Court at the Vatican. A terrace overlooking the coast at the Villa Cimbrone, Ravello, is called the Belvedere. (2) It is commonly, in gardens, a tower, deriving from the lookout towers in Italian estates placed strategically for defensive purposes. Later it served a peacetime function affording views over the surrounding countryside and might also be an attractive feature itself. Vanbrugh's Belvedere at Claremont (1715) crowns the highest point in the grounds, while Robert Adam's prospect tower at Alnwick Castle, Northumberland (Brizlee Tower), is also on a height. Alfred's Tower at Stourhead, Wiltshire, and the tower on a hill at Wimborne, Dorset, both also fulfil the criteria. A huge belvedere designed by Lord Burlington survives in poor condition at Waldershare Park, Kent. See also *Tower*.

Bengal cottage. A mid nineteenth-century summerhouse with mud walls, bamboo frames for door and window, and a reed roof. This was only one of a number of timber buildings in various

Belvedere: Claremont, Surrey.

quasi-national styles popular at the time, including the Scots cottage, the Polish hut with a roof of fir, and Russian, Danish and Swedish huts. Oriental and cottage-style buildings from the late nineteenth century made from Douglas fir with hazel inside are to be found at the Larmer Tree Gardens, Wiltshire. A 'South Seas'-type hut made from sticks and reeds was placed in an area called 'A scene in Otaheite' at Hawkstone, Shropshire, in the late eighteenth century.

Berceau (French). An arbour of trelliswork covered with creepers or climbing plants, or trees trained as an arched arbour without trellis.

Binomial system. The Latin system for classifying plants formulated by Linnaeus in his *Species Plantarum* (1753). The basic system is that the genus, or family name, comes first, followed by a second name to denote the particular species within the genus. Thus, the Scots pine is *Pinus sylvestris* and the stone pine *Pinus pinea*. A third name can be added to indicate a variety or special form of the species. The common beech is *Fagus sylvatica*, but a weeping beech is *Fagus sylvatica pendula*. Despite changes and modifications over the years, Linnaeus's system remains the basis for modern taxonomy.

Bird-cage (seventeenth/eighteenth centuries). An aviary. For garden

Border: Newby Hall, North Yorkshire.

history purposes the notion of small individual indoor cages must be banished. Birdcage Walk in St James's Park, London, is so called because it once formed a way beside which an aviary ran. A print of Chiswick, Middlesex, has a captioned bird-cage that includes an open area where fowl are seen moving about freely. The 'bird-cage' arbour at Melbourne Hall, Derbyshire, resembles a cage in appearance but was not used as such.

Boathouse. A shelter for boats beside a lake or river. Some particularly attractive and striking boathouses have been created, such as the beautiful rococo octagon at Enville, Staffordshire (c.1750), now lost. The derelict domed boathouse at Fonthill, Wiltshire (c.1750), has frostwork decoration. A large building with wings incorporating boathouses at Syon House, Middlesex (1803), has been converted into a private dwelling.

Bog garden. A soft, marshy garden, often peat-based. Water- and peat-loving plants are grown there: the finest bog gardens are at Savill Gardens, Windsor, Berkshire.

Bollard. An upright post of cast iron, wood, stone or concrete, usually standing in series, sometimes with a chain linking them. The purpose is to exclude traffic from certain areas of the garden.

Border. A long bed, usually alongside a wall or hedge. Herbaceous borders are those planted with perennial flowers and plants: among

numerous examples are the central descending lawn and borders
at Newby Hall, North Yorkshire. Cultivating borders in the
nineteenth century was initially seen as reviving seventeenth-century
practice, but, through development and interest in mixing and
massing, nineteenth- and twentieth-century borders have a vitality
and effect of their own. The ribbon border (Victorian) was a long,
narrow bed arranged in continuous lines of single colours, e.g.
blue, yellow and scarlet at Trentham Park, Staffordshire.

Bosco (Italian). A planted grove with walks; Italian Renaissance
precursor of the French bosquet. An area of shade and retreat, it
was often composed of evergreen ilex. Sometimes there is an air
of reverence or mystery, as in the 'sacro bosco' at Bomarzo.

Bosquet (French). A planted grove or shrubbery either in solid
blocks (usually of the same species) or cut through by walks.
See *Wilderness* for the English equivalent.

Botanic garden. Gardens 'for the study of plants' have existed in
England from 1621 (Oxford). The most famous of all, Kew, Surrey,
combines serious scientific organisation with attractive display,
making it an extremely popular site for visitors. Many botanic
gardens were developed in the nineteenth century as a consequence
of the ever growing number of plant introductions from abroad.

Bothy. Simple cottage, especially for young, single gardeners. In
the nineteenth and early twentieth centuries many had a reputation

Botanic garden: Logan Botanic Garden, Dumfries and Galloway.

Bowling alley: Berkeley Castle, Gloucestershire.

for primitive, cramped and squalid conditions. Often they were built along a wall of the kitchen garden. Modern bothies are still simple but much more comfortable.

Boulingrin (French). The word is a corruption of 'bowling green' but does not refer to playing bowls. It is a sunken lawn bounded by sloping banks and may be either all turf or decorated with broderie and plate-bande work (q.v.). An example is the boulingrin designed for St Germain-en-Laye.

Bower. A covered enclosure or recess in a garden; an arbour.

Bowling alley. A narrow strip for the game of ninepins (skittles). An example is at Berkeley Castle, Gloucestershire.

Bowling green. Bowling greens have featured in gardens since the middle ages. Intended to be functional, some remain today as purely decorative level lawns, such as at Claremont, Surrey, or Wentworth Castle, South Yorkshire (both eighteenth century).

Bridge. Although of practical use, in spanning a stretch of water or a road, bridges in English gardens became progressively more ornamental in the seventeenth and eighteenth centuries, to the extent of a 'dummy' bridge at Kenwood, London. The architectural style varied considerably: there are classical bridges at Chatsworth, Derbyshire, and Weston Park, Staffordshire (James Paine), Chiswick, Middlesex (James Wyatt), and Clumber Park, Nottinghamshire (attributed to Stephen Wright), while simple rustic bridges of wood with a diagonal criss-cross design abound.

Palladian bridges are a category of their own: the simplest structure is the timber bridge illustrated in Woollett's 1760 engraving of Painshill, Surrey, while the stone bridge at Stourhead, Wiltshire, is based on Palladio's bridge at Vicenza and that at Castle Howard, North Yorkshire, on his work at Rimini. But the

Bridge: Lion bridge, Burghley House, Lincolnshire.

Bridge: Palladian bridge, Wilton House, Wiltshire.

Bust: Temple of British Worthies, Stowe, Buckinghamshire.

most elaborate and beautiful are those with colonnaded superstructures, namely that at Wilton House, Wiltshire (1735-7), and its copies at Prior Park, Avon, and Stowe, Buckinghamshire. A smaller copy once existed at Hagley, Worcestershire, and another at Amesbury, Wiltshire. Vanbrugh's bridge at Blenheim, Oxfordshire, was also originally intended to have a superstructure. Bridges may affect the way water is shaped. They may also fulfil a symbolic function, as for instance in Japanese gardens, where they may link two conceptually distinct areas.

Broad-leaved. Having broad leaves not needles; with few exceptions, deciduous.

Broderie. See *Parterre de broderie*.

Brownian. Exhibiting the characteristics of 'Capability' Brown's style of landscape gardening. Brown was pre-eminent in the period 1750-80, during which he established a reputation for working to a recognisable pattern. The elements were: rolling green slopes and lawns that came up to the house; trees dotted about singly or in clumps, particularly on hills; a perimeter belt of trees; a boundary drive; a lake of natural appearance in the middle ground. Brown had many followers who adopted his style.

Buffet d'eau (French). A garden fountain shaped as a stepped table, with the water falling into a basin.

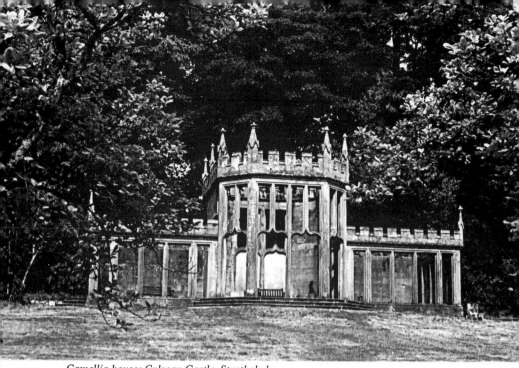

Camellia house: Culzean Castle, Strathclyde.

Bust. A sculpture of the head, shoulders and chest. In gardens, they are frequently found in niches and on pedestals.

Cabinet (French). A compartment or arbour.

Cabinet de verdure (French). A small compartment within a bosquet or one bounded by clipped hedges.

Cacti house. A glasshouse for the cultivation of cacti and succulents. They are often found as special features within larger collections at botanic gardens.

Camellia house. The popularity of the camellia and its many hybrids coincided with the rise of Victorian greenhouses and conservatories; and camellia houses, with their large windows that could be opened in summer, were built specifically to foster the plants. Examples are at Bodnant in Gwynedd, Stratfield Saye in Hampshire, Wentworth Woodhouse in South Yorkshire, and Woburn Abbey in Bedfordshire. The need for them disappeared when it was realised that camellias were able to grow outdoors throughout the year.

Camera obscura. A small portable box containing lenses and mirrors which projected the image of a scene outside on to a surface opposite the opening, where it could be traced by an artist. It was in use from the sixteenth century. See also *Claude glass*.

Campagna (Italian). A term for the open countryside. It is used in particular with reference to paintings of imagined classical Roman landscape such as was depicted by Claude Lorraine, Nicolas

Poussin and Gaspard Dughet, who influenced many designers of eighteenth-century landscape gardens in Britain. Horace Walpole used the anglicised form 'champaign'.

Canal. In gardens, an artificial sheet of water, usually rectangular in shape. The purpose may be functional (as a reservoir) as well as decorative, but the latter usage is particularly marked in formal gardens of the grand French manner. In Britain the Long Water at Hampton Court, Middlesex, is a notable instance of a dominating canal on a main axis relating to the house; smaller, but no less attractive, examples are at Erddig, Clwyd; Westbury Court, Gloucestershire; and Wrest Park, Bedfordshire. An unusual slanting T-shaped canal is at Bramham, West Yorkshire.

Canopy. The cover afforded by the uppermost or broadest branches of trees in a wood when in leaf.

Carpet bedding (primarily Victorian). The practice of forming beds of low-growing foliage plants, all of an even height, in patterns that resemble a carpet both in the intricacy of their design and in the uniformity of surface. Flowers were gradually admitted, reluctantly at first. It was introduced by John Fleming at Cliveden, Buckinghamshire, in 1868 and has continued to be employed, especially in public parks. Designs can vary from geometrical to images and lettered inscriptions.

Canal: Erddig, Clwyd.

Canal: Schönbusch, Aschaffenburg, Bavaria, Germany.

Cascade. A fall of water, natural or, more often in gardens, artificial. There are magnificent examples in several of the great Italian Renaissance villa gardens, as at Villa Lante or Villa Aldobrandini, which were followed by many others all over Europe and in Russia. In England there were few formal cascades – the best-known is at Chatsworth, Derbyshire – but Brown created some naturalistic ones, e.g. at Blenheim, Oxfordshire, and Ashburnham, East Sussex, while nature was given a helping hand

Cascade: Chatsworth, Derbyshire.

by means of strategically arranged rocks for the series of cascades at Hackfall, North Yorkshire.

Casino, casina. An ornamental pavilion. The word is Italian but has been applied to a number of buildings in English gardens, e.g. the now lost casina at Chiswick, Middlesex, a tall building with a lantern (before 1717), and the casino at Wilton, Wiltshire (by Sir William Chambers, pre-1759). Chambers also built a neo-classical casino at Marino, Dublin, in the plan of a Greek cross.

Casino: Marino, Dublin, Ireland.

Casita (Spanish=small house). A small pavilion in loggia form. Harold Peto constructed one at his terraced garden of Iford Manor, Wiltshire.

Castellation. Decoration in the form of turrets and battlements, like a castle. In gardens some Gothic buildings and mock castles exhibit these features. There is much castellated work at Castle Howard, North Yorkshire.

Cast iron. See under *Ironwork*.

Castle. Castles have long been perceived as romantic and desirable objects in a landscape garden. In some instances, as with ruined abbeys, real castles, either whole or derelict, might form part of the view (e.g. Chepstow Castle at Piercefield, Gwent), but in the eighteenth century a spate of sham castles appeared, ranging from Vanbrugh's fortifications at Castle Howard, North Yorkshire, in the 1720s, to Stainborough Castle, Wentworth, South Yorkshire (1729), and Sanderson Miller's deliberately ruined castles at Hagley, Worcestershire (1747), and Wimpole, Cambridgeshire (c.1770 but designed earlier).

Catena d'acqua (Italian Renaissance). An artificial cascade in a series of elaborately decorated steps and carried in an edged channel (literally 'chain of water'). Two superb examples are at the Villa Lante and the Villa Caprarola.

Cemetery garden. The modern cemetery dates from the early nineteenth century, and the Victorian cemeteries were laid out in a number of garden styles: informal, with winding walks and clumps; more formal, with straight walks; and purely symmetrical, which permitted a tighter disposition of graves. Loudon made particular use of conifers, but there was a later reaction to the sombre effect created, and flowers and broad-leaved trees appeared. George Loddiges planted up Abney Park, London, as an arboretum (1840).

Charmille (French). A tall, clipped hedge.

Chinese. With a garden tradition stretching back longer than that

Casita: Iford Manor, Wiltshire.

Castle: Hagley Hall, Worcestershire.

of any other nation, there is no such thing as a typical Chinese garden. However, the dominant elements are rocks and water: rocks are often piled up to form artificial crags, and their hardness contrasts and harmonises with the soft, reflective water. The visitor passes through the garden as if on a journey, experiencing incidents and features from different angles, even within a small area, by means of contrasts (high and low levels, light and shade). Trees are valued for their symbolic associations and plants for their scents.

Chinoiserie. A westernised version of Chinese motifs and designs. In English gardens, from Richard Bateman's Chinese houses and decorations in the 1730s the taste spread so rapidly that by the 1750s Horace Walpole was moved to complain at the number of Chinese buildings. One or two were claimed to be authentic in design, such as the Chinese House at Shugborough, Staffordshire, but for the most part buildings exhibited upturned eaves, bells and dragon finials in a way that had little to do with the real China. Chinoiserie also coloured the designs of garden furniture and bridges (the commonly found criss-cross pattern). Sir William Chambers's pagoda at Kew, Surrey, is the best-known survivor. Among much chinoiserie in Europe may be mentioned the Chinese Tea House at Sanssouci, Germany.

Cistern. Used in gardens for collecting and storing rainwater, cisterns were usually rectangular in shape and made of lead or cast iron, though in Roman gardens they were generally of stone. Decoration, cast from moulds, with friezes or panels, was often elaborate. Most English examples date from after 1600. An eighteenth-century lead cistern with panels, heraldic devices and figures is at Sackville College, East Grinstead, West Sussex.

Clairvoie. An openwork gate, fence or grille at the end of an allée which permits a view to the scenery beyond. They are often

Clairvoie: screen by Tijou, Hampton Court, Middlesex.

found as panels in a wall, as at Westbury Court, Gloucestershire. One in gate form stands at the end of the long walk beside the walled garden at Castle Howard, North Yorkshire. A complete screen of railings may also be referred to as a clairvoie, such as Tijou's remarkable work of repoussé wrought iron at Hampton Court, Middlesex, or the gate screen at Leeswood, Clwyd.

Classical. A term usually applied to buildings (especially temples) in a Greek or Roman style. See *Temple* and *Orders of architecture*.

Claude glass. A small black convex glass used for reflecting landscape views in miniature, named after the painter Claude Lorraine. The resulting image would show broad tonal values but not detail or colour. A silvered glass was used in dull weather. They were popular in the seventeenth and eighteenth centuries, particularly among those who were in search of the Picturesque.

Cloche. A glass under which plants are forced; a frame.

Cloister garden. An ornamental garden within the cloisters of medieval monasteries. However, no firm evidence has been found for their existence, and it is more likely that a stretch of grass occupied the cloister area, with recreational and herb gardens outside.

Clone. One of a number of genetically identical organisms produced from a single organism.

Close walk. A secluded walk, often between tall hedges.

Clump. A number of trees planted together to form a distinct group. William Kent designed layouts at Euston Hall, Suffolk, and Holkham, Norfolk, where there were several clumps forming a pattern, decried by Horace Walpole as resembling the ten of spades. Kent planted tightly on purpose, the idea being that the weaker trees would be weeded out as the clumps grew. 'Capability' Brown is the most famous exponent of clumps, his favourite motif being to place clumps of beech on top of hills and slopes, as at Petworth, West Sussex.

Coade stone. An artificial ceramic resembling natural limestone. It was produced by Mrs Eleanor Coade in her kilns at Lambeth, London, from 1769, and the factory continued in operation until 1843. Thousands of pieces were produced, including urns, terms, sundials, finials, fountains and figures. Among countless examples may be singled out the river god at Ham House, Surrey; the Triton fountain at Petworth, West Sussex; the Borghese vase and pedestal at Wrest Park, Bedfordshire; and, most extraordinary of all, the umbrello at Great Saxham Hall, Suffolk.

Cock pit. An area for cock-fighting. The pit at Nostell Priory, West Yorkshire, has been partly turned into a pond but the grass bank seating survives.

Clump: Blenheim Palace, Oxfordshire.

*Coade stone: Druid at Shugborough,
Staffordshire.*

Cock pit: Nostell Priory, West Yorkshire.

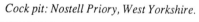

Cold bath: plunge bath, Packwood House, Warwickshire.

Column: the Grenville Column, Stowe, Buckinghamshire

Conservative wall: Chatsworth, Derbyshire.

Cold bath. A bath in the grounds, usually on the site of a spring. Greville noted in 1818 that the bath in the grotto at Oatlands, Surrey, was 'as clear as crystal and as cold as ice'. Often a bath house would be associated with the bath.

College garden. The gardens at Oxford and Cambridge are major glories of both universities. There are many remnants of old features, such as the Mount at New College, Oxford. Many college gardens are laid out in a formal style of lawns, walks and borders; Worcester College, Oxford, however, has a nineteenth-century picturesque garden with lake. In Cambridge several gardens (the Backs) have the advantage of the river running past.

Colonnade. A row of columns or, by transference, a similar arrangement in green materials.

Columbarium. See *Dovecote.*

Column. A tall pillar, often surmounted by a figure and set at a distance from the house. The purpose is generally commemorative. They are commonly found in eighteenth-century landscaped gardens. From many examples, the Column of Liberty at Gibside, Tyne and Wear, makes a political point.

Compartiment (French). Patterned bed with the design created by a single material, usually box. See also *Parterre de compartiment.*

Compartment. A distinct area within a garden, sometimes fenced or hedged; a room.

Conceit. A charming, delightful or whimsical object (building or other structure) in a garden. It might be unexpected or illogical, such as a small bridge over grass.

Conduit. A channel or pipe (wood, brick, etc) for conducting water.

Coniferous. Cone-bearing, especially evergreens (pines, firs), often contrasted with deciduous.

Conservative wall (Victorian). A wall against which glass cases to house camellias, etc, are sheltered, as at Chatsworth, Derbyshire (by Paxton) and at Somerleyton Hall, Suffolk.

Conservatory. A glasshouse for protecting (conserving) tender plants. Often synonymous with orangery or greenhouse, the conservatory would in the seventeenth and eighteenth centuries be free-standing, but in the nineteenth it could alternatively be attached to the house. Fine conservatories survive at Syon House, Middlesex (1830), and Bicton, Devon.

Conservatory: Syon House, Middlesex.

Corbeille: Calke Abbey, Derbyshire.

Coquillage: Goldney, Bristol, Avon.

Coppice. A tree, or wood, cut down to a low stump a few inches from the ground (known as a coppice stool) every few years so that a number of long, slender uprights grow from the single stool. These can be used for firewood, hurdles or thatching. This system of woodland management, common in medieval times, is less often encountered now.

Coquillage. Use or display of shellwork, often in shell rooms or grottoes. It can also form a decorative motif such as in Thomas Robins's borders for his watercolours of eighteenth-century rococo gardens.

Corbeille. A flower bed edged with wicker basketwork. Repton designed a large one for Courteenhall, Northamptonshire, in 1791 and several for the lawns at the Royal Pavilion, Brighton, East Sussex (1805). The edging may also be of interlaced wrought-iron hoops or terra-cotta. A refinement was the 'Hardenberg basket', a basketwork container 2.5 metres in diameter set in the middle of a small flower parterre.

Corinthian. See *Orders of architecture.*

Cornucopia (literally 'horn of plenty'). A large horn overflowing with fruit and produce. In some gardens it could be built up as a wooden structure of 2 metres or more which would be filled with plants and flowers, as at Muskau, Germany.

Coronary garden. A garden for flowers that could be cut and woven into garlands.

Cottage garden. A garden attached to a cottage where the planting is informal, apparently artless, crowded with flowers, vegetables and fruit trees, with trailers, climbers and creepers on the woodwork.

Cottage orné. (1) A consciously contrived rustic cottage for decoration (as well as habitation) in a park, usually of the Picturesque period. A cluster was built at Blaise Hamlet, Bristol (1811).

(2) A luxurious second home, an occasional country residence, such as at Endsleigh, Devon.

Coupe de gazon. See *Gazon coupé*.

Courtyard garden. A garden within surrounding walls or buildings. Courtyard gardens vary considerably in style and arrangement, according to the size and amount of direct sunlight. Particularly good examples can be found at Montacute House, Somerset (from

Cottage orné: Endsleigh, Devon.

Cottage garden: Anne Hathaway's Cottage, Shottery, Warwickshire.

the late sixteenth century); Cotehele, Cornwall (originally Tudor); Sissinghurst, Kent (revived after 1930).

Cover. (1) The spread created by trees (cf. *Canopy*).
(2) Ground cover: low plants and shrubs growing in a wood, or covering an area instead of grass.

Crazy paving. A pavement or path composed of irregular pieces of stone.

Crenellation. An indented parapet or battlement, often used in gardens for the decoration of Gothic buildings, for example the Gothic Seat at Painswick, Gloucestershire. See also *Castellation*.

Crinkle-crankle wall (or crinkum-crankum). A serpentine wall, with fruit grown in the bays. An example is at Heveningham Hall, Suffolk, designed by Brown.

Cromlech. Originally a burial chamber, but in gardens usually an upright stone circle (cf. *Druid temple*). One of the grottoes at Fonthill, Wiltshire, has been described as an imitation of a cromlech, and another example is at Glynllifon, Gwynedd.

Cultivar. A variety of plant that has been developed and maintained by cultivation.

Cut work (European Renaissance). A pattern of small flower beds separated by narrow paths in a parterre.

Daedalus. A labyrinth.

Dairy. Dairies which were functional could nonetheless be incorporated into 'village picturesque' scenes in an estate, e.g. the Hameau (q.v.) at Versailles. There is a delightful thatched dairy by John Nash at Blaise, Bristol, while James Wyatt's dairy at Cobham Hall, Kent (1795), resembles a chapel. Henry Holland designed a Chinese dairy (1789) at Woburn Abbey, Bedfordshire.

Dam. Controlling and shaping water by means of dams has been one of the most powerful tools of the landscape designer. Henry Hoare created the lakescape at Stourhead, Wiltshire, by damming several pools, and the superb lake at Blenheim, Oxfordshire, is the result of 'Capability' Brown's judicious damming of the river Glyme.

Danish hut. See under *Bengal cottage.*

Deciduous. Trees or shrubs that shed their leaves (as opposed to evergreens).

Crenellation: Gothic seat, Painswick Rococo Garden, Gloucestershire.

(Below right) *Crinkle-crankle wall: Deans Court, Wimborne, Dorset.*

Dairy: Blaise, Bristol, Avon.

*Deercote:
Bishop
Auckland,
County
Durham.*

*Deer house: Chiswick
House, Middlesex.*

*Deer park:
Boughton
Monchelsea
Place, Kent.*

Deercote, deer pen (also shed, shelter). A building for the shelter
and protection of deer, especially in winter. A magnificent example
is the arcaded deercote at Bishop Auckland, County Durham,
attributed to Thomas Wright. A deer shelter under a ha-ha is at
Londesborough, Humberside, and a deershed has been rebuilt at
Wentworth Woodhouse, South Yorkshire.

Deer house. A building for sheltering deer. There was a pair at
Chiswick, Middlesex (c.1720), one of which survives, attributed
to Lord Burlington or possibly Colen Campbell. The deer paddock
stood adjacent to them, separated from the gardens by a ha-ha.

Deer park. A large park for keeping deer. In medieval times the
prime purpose was hunting, and the park would sometimes be
surrounded with a ditch and have entrances known as 'deer leaps'
by which the deer could enter but not leave.

Dipping well: Hestercombe House, Somerset.

Dell. A hollow, or small valley, usually well planted; hence a dell garden.

Demesne. A house and its land; an estate. The term is more common in Ireland.

Dipping well or pool. A small pool, half vaulted over, below a terrace. It would be fed by a wall fountain, and in turn it would feed further pools at lower levels. Great use of dipping wells was made by Edwin Lutyens, at the Deanery Garden, Berkshire; Hestercombe, Somerset; and Abbotswood, Gloucestershire, among others. The origin of the term is that they were used for filling watering-cans.

Doric. See *Orders of architecture*.

Dovecote. A building for the rearing and habitation of doves (similarly a pigeon house for pigeons), bred for food from the

Dovecote: Felbrigg Hall, Norfolk.

middle ages. Particularly good examples are to be seen at Athelhampton, Dorset; Cotehele, Cornwall; Priory Garden, Dunster, Somerset; and Rousham, Oxfordshire. Columbarium is the Latin name sometimes used for dovecote. In Scotland the form 'doocot' is found.

Drive. A route around but within a park, intended originally for horse-drawn carriages. Humphry Repton devised a number of long and intricate drives, from which much of the scenery could be seen. In his Red Book for Blaise Castle, Bristol (1796), he explained that 'In the drive which I have marked out from the house to the castle, I shall avail myself of that vista thro' the wood towards the river, which has always been considered as one of the striking features of the place .... that the most careless observer may have leisure to view the delightful scene, and before he quits the spot entirely the whole expanse of water, of shipping, and distant mountains will pass before the eye.' See also *Approach*, *Riding* and *Walk*.

Druid's cell or cave. The name given to some rustic structures or hermitages in the eighteenth century, when there was considerable antiquarian interest in the Druids. An example is the Druid's Cell (also called the Hermitage) at Stourhead, Wiltshire.

Druid temple. A circle of upright stones in the manner of Stonehenge. One was erected at Piercefield, Gwent (post-1750); the supreme example was at Ilton, North Yorkshire (1820s).

Dug work (late seventeenth/early eighteenth century). Patterns of flower beds.

Dutch. The elements of the traditional Dutch style (seventeenth century) represent an adaptation and modification of French formal ideas. Dutch gardens tended to be flat and compact, with an emphasis on small canals, hedges, topiary, lead statuary and flowering bulbs and shrubs. There are, however, one or two examples on the grand scale, such as the restored palace gardens at Het Loo. Westbury Court, Gloucestershire, gives a good idea of the Dutch style as employed in England.

Dyke (Scottish). Low wall of stones, turf, etc., to create an enclosure.

Eagle's cage. See *Aviary*.

Earthwork. An embankment or work of excavation and building up of earth.

Edging. Edgings can be used to delineate paths or to surround flower beds. They can be either openwork (hooped wood, iron, wire or basketwork) or solid curbs (boards, brick, stone). Special tiles or bricks (pianelle) were used for edging Italian flower gardens. Edging tiles are sometimes rope-topped. Timber edging rails

Dovecote: doocot at Mertoun Gardens, Borders.

Egyptian garden: Biddulph Grange, Staffordshire.

Druid temple:
Ilton, North Yorkshire.

are described for 'fret' gardens in John Rea's *Flora* (1665).

Egyptian garden. A garden employing Egyptian architectural features, e.g. the Egyptian court, with sphinxes and a tomb-like entrance, at Biddulph Grange, Staffordshire (c.1860).

Elysium (mythological, the dwelling place of the fortunate dead). A place of delight. The Elysian Fields form part of an elaborate scheme at Stowe, Buckinghamshire.

Embankment. A bank or mount built up to protect or to give a view from. In gardens embankments were often created from the spoil of excavated lakes (e.g. at Chiswick, Middlesex) and formed

Exedra: Belton House, Lincolnshire.

Exedra: Painswick Rococo Garden, Gloucestershire.

into a terrace walk.

Embroidery. Intricate designs comparable to those produced in needlework, forming patterns in turf or beds. See *Parterre de broderie* and *Gazon coupé*.

English landscape garden. See *Landscape garden*.

Entrelacs (French). A design of interconnecting bands. See also *Knot garden*.

Espalier. A fruit tree (sometimes in a row) whose branches are trained flat against a wall or frame, which itself can be called an espalier. They are very common: a good example is at Westbury Court, Gloucestershire.

Estrade (French = low platform). There is a special sense in which the word is used to refer to the clipping and training of trees in medieval Burgundy to create level tiers of branches in the manner of a cake-stand.

Étang (French). A small lake.

Étoile (French = star). A 'circus' or meeting of straight walks in a forest. See *Rondpoint*.

Exedra. In gardens, an area with a semicircular backdrop, in the manner of an apse, found particularly in the eighteenth century. At Chiswick, Middlesex, the backdrop is formed of a hedge, in front of which stood three Roman statues; at Painswick, Gloucestershire, the exedra is architectural, a curving Gothic screen. An extraordinary curving hedge arcade shaped to form an exedra was once at Hartwell House, Buckinghamshire.

Exotic. A species which originates in another country, i.e. is not native to the land in which it is being grown.

Extensive gardening. See *Forest gardening*.

Eyecatcher. A feature placed on a distant eminence (but not necessarily on the owner's property). The best-known is the façade erected by William Kent in a field opposite the garden of Rousham, Oxfordshire (1730s); another excellent example is the pinnacled façade at Creech Grange, Dorset (1740). Many buildings placed on a height remote from the house, like some of Sanderson Miller's castles or Robert Adam's temple at Audley End, Essex, can be regarded as eyecatchers.

Fabrique (French). Ornamental building in a garden (especially eighteenth century) often with cultural or emotional associations.

Ferme ornée (French = ornamented farm). A garden in which an operational farm is included in the overall design and where the farm both contributes to the effect and is itself planted up with ornamental trees and hedgerows. Although the term is French, the genre is predominantly English, with early eighteenth-century examples at Riskins Park, Buckinghamshire, and Dawley, Middlesex, being superseded by the great fermes ornées of the Leasowes, West Midlands, and Woburn Farm, Surrey. At the latter, Whately tells us (1770) that out of 150 acres (60 hectares), 35 were cultivated as pleasure grounds, the remainder being two-thirds pasture and one-third arable, but that the 'decorations' were carried through all parts by means of a broad belt walk lined with colourful shrubs, trees and hedges.

Fernery. (1) An outdoor collection of ferns, or the area in which they are grown.
(2) A glasshouse built to house and protect ferns imported from warm countries. The fernery is essentially a product of the mid-Victorian passion for collecting ferns. A survivor is at Tatton Park, Cheshire.

Fig house. Greenhouse for growing figs, as at Raby Castle, County Durham.

Finial. An ornament placed on top of a roof, pinnacle, pediment, arch or column. It is an exceedingly common decoration in gardens

– on gate piers, arches, columns, balustrades, garden buildings, walls and pedestals. Particularly popular forms are the pineapple, the obelisk and the ball (pommel). Vases and urns may serve the same function as finials. A finial may stand by itself, as at Arley Hall, Cheshire.

Fishing pavilion. A waterside building from which one could fish. Various styles of architecture were used, as they were for other garden buildings, and Humphry Repton designed a number. Jeffry Wyatville designed a Chinese Fishing Temple at Virginia Water, Surrey, in the 1820s. Perhaps the most remarkable essay was Robert Adam's Fishing Room at Kedleston Hall, Derbyshire (1771), which incorporates a boathouse and cold bath. See *Tabernacle*.

Fishpond. A pond in which fish are stocked: it may vary from a formal stone basin to a pool sometimes derived from an old stewpond (q.v.).

Flintwork. Flint facing for walls and buildings has often been used in gardens. It plays a prominent part in dressing many of the buildings at West Wycombe, Buckinghamshire.

Floral clock. The floral clock is a twentieth-century feature found in public parks and seaside resorts. The face of the clock is planted out with low-growing flowers and plants, with the moving hands also covered with small foliage.

Finial: Erddig, Clwyd.

Fig house: Raby Castle, County Durham.

Flintwork: Temple of the Winds, West Wycombe, Buckingham- shire.

Florilegium (Latin = collection of flowers). In literature, an anthology, but in garden history it has a specific meaning from the seventeenth century to denote a book of engraved illustrations of garden flowers and ornamental plants. The first was Emanuel Sweerts' *Florilegium*, 1612.

Florist. A cultivator or seller of flowers, or a student of flowers or flora.

Florists' societies. From early in the eighteenth century florists'

Folly: Shobden Arches, Herefordshire.

societies were formed to exhibit flowers and compete for prizes. The so-called 'florists' flowers' grown by specialists were pinks, carnations, tulips, hyacinths, auriculas, anemones, polyanthus and ranunculus.

Flower garden. A garden in which flower beds form the focal point. The beds can be regular or irregular, like William Mason's serpentine and kidney-shaped beds in the lawn at Nuneham Courtenay, Oxfordshire (c.1770).

Flowery meads (medieval). A clover lawn or rich meadow sown with different sorts of flowers. A modern equivalent is the meadow deliberately planted with wild flowers, as at Holker Hall, Cumbria.

Flue wall. See *Heated wall.*

Fog house (Scottish). A summerhouse lined with moss (fog = moss).

Folly. In gardens, a structure that demonstrates eccentricity or excess rather than practical purpose: it may have been expensive, bizarre in design or with no apparent function or meaning. The eighteenth-century landscape garden is the arena in which follies flourished most readily, although they are not unknown in the twentieth century. They demand attention and were intended to impress, puzzle or just give pleasure. They can take many forms – sham castles, ruins, towers, grottoes, hermits' cells. One of the most extravagant is the giant stone Pineapple at Dunmore, Central Region, Scotland.

Forcing. The speeding of a plant's growth to maturity or ripeness by means of, for example, a frame.

Forest gardening. Also called 'extensive gardening', this was an approach advocated by Stephen Switzer (early eighteenth century) which unified the whole estate by means of great axial lines, and in particular brought forest plantation, though well away from the house, into the overall scheme. Cirencester Park, Gloucestershire, demonstrates his precepts best, with two enormous woods being yoked ('willing woods', as Pope called them) by means of the 5 mile (8 km) avenue to Sapperton.

Forest lawn. A clearing in a wood, often used as pasture. The forest lawn dates back to medieval times and is identifiable with the 'laund' or 'lawnde' of the pastoral poets. William Gilpin (1724-1804) made much of the idea, with particular reference to the New Forest, Hampshire, where horses or ponies would graze in open spaces which had bushes of thorn, gorse, etc spreading into them. This combination of 'drifting' bushes and uneven lawn or ground was adapted in the shrubberies of Regency gardens (q.v.).

Form. The smallest subdivision of plants, based on minor characteristics (e.g. colour of petals).

Formal. Regular, linear, geometrical in design. Formality is most closely associated with the traditional French, Italian and Dutch styles.

Formal: the parterre at Villandry, France.

Fountain: Ascott, Buckinghamshire.

Fountain. Fountains may consist of jets of water into the air or of structures sometimes with elaborate groupings of figures from which or over which water pours. They have played a key part in gardens since Roman times. The Italian Renaissance was perhaps their heyday in terms of fine sculpture, hydraulic engineering and iconography, which coalesced at places such as Villa d'Este, Tivoli. An astonishing array of fountains was also to be found at Versailles. Generally water had to come from a reservoir at a higher level, in order to create the necessary flow and pressure, before the advent of modern mechanical and electrical motors. Many group sculpture fountains were made in Britain during the Victorian period, e.g. at Kinmel Park, Clwyd.

Frame. A glass cover for protecting plants.

French. The French traditional style has much in common with the Italian and derived many ideas from it. The characteristics of a grand French garden are: a parterre or series of parterres adjacent to the house, with flowers and plants in regular beds, and fountains; stonework, balustrades and statuary; formal basins and canals, with cascades; away from the house a bosquet with walks cut through it; and long, broad avenues forming a grid pattern, with straight or diagonal axes leading back to the house. The archetype of this scheme is Versailles.

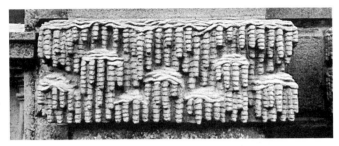

Frostwork: Banqueting House, Studley Royal, North Yorkshire.

Fret. A geometrical pattern of flower beds described by John Rea in *Flora* (1665).

Frostwork. A type of rusticated decoration where bands of stone are carved to appear like icicles. The Banqueting House at Studley Royal, North Yorkshire (1730), has such decoration.

Fruit garden. An orchard; an area where fruit trees are grown.

Fruit store. A building for the storage of picked fruit, as at Newhailes, Lothian.

Galerie (French). An arcade looking over a garden.

Gallery. An arched tunnel with plants trained over it: cf. *Pergola*, *Berceau*.

Game larder. A small building for the hanging of game. Although functional, it can be of architectural interest, e.g. Sanderson Miller's

Game larder: House of Dun, Tayside.

hexagonal game larder at Farnborough Hall, Warwickshire (1750s). Samuel Wyatt's octagonal yellow brick larder at Holkham Hall, Norfolk (c.1780), has walls lined with English alabaster for coolness, above a room with a well.

Garden. An area cultivated for the growth of flowers, shrubs, trees and lawn (though the raked-earth Japanese gardens may be plantless). It is bordered or enclosed: the word is cognate with 'yard'.

Gardeners' tunnel. A tunnel connecting the gardeners' basic working area (kitchen, garden, etc) with the ornamental gardens: the purpose was to shield the owners or visitors from seeing those who did the work. There is one at Cobham Hall, Kent, but the prize must go to the tunnel at Calke Abbey, Derbyshire, which extends for approximately 70 metres.

Gardenesque. A term coined by J. C. Loudon in 1832 for a style that allowed each plant to develop naturally and fully and to be displayed to its best advantage, i.e. the garden became plant-centred rather than plants being forced into a preconceived design. The concept was, however, modified, if not distorted, by later authors such as Edward Kemp (1850), who defined it as seeking beauty of lines and variety – mixed and irregular.

Garth (medieval). A garden or yard.

Gate: Chirk Castle, Clwyd.

Gate. The gate to a park or estate may range from a simple wooden construction to a fine-quality wrought-iron piece as in many seventeenth- or eighteenth-century estates.

Gatehouse (medieval to sixteenth century). An ornamental structure over a gate near the house, often in a courtyard, as at Charlecote Park, Warwickshire.

Gate pier. The upright at each side of an entrance gate. They may be decorative, often in keeping with the architecture of the house, and sometimes surmounted by a finial. There is a particularly fine series of gate piers and lodges at the seven entrances to Clumber Park, Nottinghamshire.

Gazebo. Historically a small, sometimes two-storeyed, garden pavilion which affords a good view over the garden. It was often placed at a corner angle. The jocular derivation is from quasi-Latin, 'I shall gaze'. Among many gazebos are those at Montacute House, Somerset (Elizabethan), and Westbury Court, Gloucestershire (c.1720). Modern usage, however, allows the term to cover any small arbour.

Gazon coupé (seventeenth century). Turf in which shapes have been cut out and filled with sand, coloured earth or gravel. Sometimes the turf itself would be cut into designs against a background of sand. It was found in Britain as well as France, e.g. at Chatsworth, Derbyshire, or Longleat, Wiltshire. A Victorian example is the dragon parterre at Biddulph Grange, Staffordshire, where two dragons are cut out of the turf and the shapes filled in with gravel.

Genius of the place. Alexander Pope exhorted the would-be garden designer to 'Consult the genius of the place in all', by which was meant the essential character or 'feel' of a situation. This might entail emphasising certain qualities or making deficiencies good, such as raising artificial mounts in a flat garden.

Genus. A group of closely related species. See *Binomial system*.

Geometrical. A geometrical layout is one where straight lines and circles form a pattern for paths, rows of trees or statuary, beds and water. Such designs are also referred to as regular or formal. They are well-established in traditional French and Italian gardens and were also found extensively in Britain until the early eighteenth century, when a reaction set in (see *Landscape garden*).

Giardino segreto (Italian=secret garden). An enclosed area within a garden. These compartments of retreat were often to be found in Italian gardens of the Renaissance, as in the villa gardens of Frascati, and could sometimes be quite large in scale. See also *Hortus conclusus*.

Gatehouse: Burton Agnes Hall, Humberside.

Gazebo: Westbury Court Garden, Gloucestershire.

Gate pier: Clumber Park, Nottinghamshire.

Gazebo: Montacute House, Somerset.

Gazon coupé: dragon parterre, Biddulph Grange, Staffordshire.

Giardino segreto: Villa di Monte Solare, Colle San Paolo, Tuscany, Italy.

Gothic: Gothic Temple, Stowe, Buckinghamshire.

Giochi d'acqua (Italian = water jokes). A common device in Italian Renaissance gardens, the water joke spread to other countries including England and Russia. The hapless visitor would be unexpectedly drenched from secret spouts concealed in statues or under foot. The devices would be triggered either from a distance or by the visitor's step. Italian examples include the Villa Mondragone and its neighbour the Villa Aldobrandini. The copper willow-tree fountain at Chatsworth, Derbyshire, is a successor to the late seventeenth-century original.

Glade. A clearing in a wood.

Gloriette (originally Arabic). A pavilion away from the house which could be used as a summerhouse or a lookout for defensive purposes. Queen Eleanor's gloriette (c.1280) still stands on the island at Leeds Castle, Kent. There are references to 'La Gloriette' in the grounds of Chepstow Castle, Gwent, but no details. The gloriette at the Jardin des Plantes in Paris (1788) is constructed of cast iron (a very early use of the material).

Gnome. Garden gnomes date back to nineteenth-century Germany but did not reach England until the 1890s. Lamport Hall, Northamptonshire, claims to have the first.

Goose foot. See *Patte d'oie*.

Gothic, Gothick. The Gothic revival in gardens in the eighteenth century in Britain saw the reuse of medieval features such as pointed arches, crenellation, buttresses and the ogee curve for the construction of garden buildings. In some cases there was an ideological motivation, namely to hark back to a former age of supposed virtues (e.g. the Gothic Temple at Stowe, Buckinghamshire) and also to assert a British traditional style of architecture. Many architects essayed Gothic: William Kent, James Gibbs, Sanderson Miller, Robert Adam. Horace Walpole introduced Gothic revival in houses at his famous extravaganza at Strawberry Hill, Middlesex (1748).

Gradation, graduation (eighteenth and nineteenth centuries). (1) A progressive change or transition from one colour (cf. *Shading*) or form to another.

(2) An arrangement of species in a bed with the smallest at the front and tallest at the back or in the centre.

Grafting. The inserting of a small part of a plant (scion) into a full plant (stock).

Grand Manner. The term used in France to denote large-scale seventeenth-century formal layouts and in Britain the same (cf. *Baroque*) but with awareness of the countryside and incorporating views of it.

Grass plat. See *Plat*.

Greenhouse. A building with extensive use of glass to protect plants (originally 'greens') from cold and permit them maximum sunlight. Although known from the seventeenth century, the greenhouse came into its own in the nineteenth, with the development of glass roofs. An example which has much of its original technology is at Wentworth Castle, South Yorkshire. See also *Conservatory*.

Greenhouse: Wentworth Castle, South Yorkshire.

Greenhouse corridor: Alton Towers, Staffordshire.
Grotto: Grotta del Buontalenti, Boboli gardens, Florence, Italy.

Greenhouse corridor. A glass-covered walk linking or providing access to hothouses and greenhouses. Greenhouse corridors may themselves contain climbing plants on the walls. They are found at many botanic gardens and in ranges of greenhouses as at Luton Hoo, Bedfordshire.

Greens. Evergreen trees or shrubs. Pope refers to greens in a satirical essay on topiary in *The Guardian*, 1713.

Grille. An opening in a wall to permit a view through (see also *Clairvoie*). The opening is divided by (usually) iron uprights in the manner of a gate. Among many examples is one in the walled garden at Castle Howard, North Yorkshire (garden begun 1703).

Grille: Iford Manor, Wiltshire.

Grotto. A cave-like chamber, often decorated with minerals, shells or pebbles. The sixteenth- and seventeenth-century French and Italian grottoes would be architecturally formal on the outside but inside would contain lavish ornamentation, often of a naturalistic kind. Those at Boboli, Florence, and nearby at the Villa Medici, Castello, had allegorical meanings. Water would frequently feature, as a pool, fountain or cascade. In Britain the grotto became more naturalistic outside as well as within during the eighteenth century,

Grotto: Clandon Park, Surrey.

from Stephen Wright's grotto at Claremont, Surrey (1750). Some were extravagant creations taking several years to build, such as the spar-decorated grotto at Painshill, Surrey, and the two-storey structure at Oatlands, Surrey. The most celebrated grotto-builders were the Lanes, father and son, of Tisbury, Wiltshire.

Grove. A small wood, a collection of trees grown for ornamental appearance. Common in the seventeenth century, they would at that time be geometrical in form. Designed groves could range from open to close, as defined by Philip Miller. Open groves had large shady trees, whose branches provided a canopy, and might be planted irregularly. Close groves had some large trees but were underplanted with shrubs or small trees, making the walks private. A grove is often synonymous with a bosquet or wilderness (q.v.).

Guglio. A column in pyramid form which acts as a spouting fountain, the water running down the sides. Vanbrugh designed one for the great basin at Stowe, Buckinghamshire (c.1715), but it has long since been destroyed and the stonework reused.

Guns and cannon. These can be used as garden ornaments, sometimes mounted on a carriage. Examples are at Goldney, Bristol, and Hever Castle, Kent.

Ha-ha. A sunk ditch, invisible from more than a few yards away, which divides the garden from pasture land outside. The purpose was to 'call in the country', to bring the fields into the garden and unify the two in design terms. The construction was as illustrated, with a retaining wall of brick or stone on the garden side and a sloping bank on the pasture side. This prevented cattle from getting into the garden. The device was in widespread use in the eighteenth century. The name derives from the cry of exclamation (it should be 'aha') as one comes unexpectedly upon the ditch. The concept is

Ha-ha: Gilbert White's garden, Selborne, Hampshire.

Heated wall: boiler houses and heated wall, Whitworth Hall, County Durham.

Hedge: Westbury Court Garden, Gloucestershire.

described by Dezallier d'Argenville but was popularised in its recognisable English form by Charles Bridgeman and many others. The ha-ha at Rousham, Oxfordshire, still fulfils its original function.

Hameau (French = hamlet). A group of rural buildings (mill, dairy, etc) to form a 'toy village' such as Marie-Antoinette created in a corner of the estate at Versailles (1785).

Hanging garden. A garden planted in a series of rising terraces, as most famously in ancient Babylon.

Hanging wood. A term used most commonly in connection with the English landscape garden. It may refer to a wood that crowns a hill, or, more often, to a wood that hangs on the side of a hill. It was generally agreed that it was desirable to look at the wood from below, preferably so that the brow of the hill was not visible. There is a hanging wood at Selborne, Hampshire, opposite Gilbert White's house and garden.

Hardenberg basket. See *Corbeille*.

Hardy plant. One that can survive outdoors all year.

Heated wall. A wall in a flower or kitchen garden which contains conduits or pipes for heating the wall. An example, with its boiler houses, is at Whitworth Hall, County Durham.

Heath house. See under *Moss hut*.

Hedge. A line of tightly growing trees or shrubs to delineate a boundary or act as a screen within a garden. It may be composed

Herb garden: Kentwell Hall, Suffolk.

Hermitage: Stowe, Buckinghamshire.

Herm: Chiswick House, Middlesex.

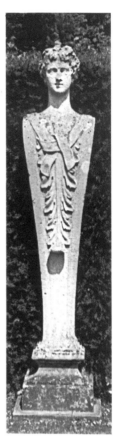

of a wide range of species, both evergreen and deciduous. Favourite evergreens have included box, holly, ilex, laurel, laurustinus, privet and yew; and deciduous, beech, hornbeam and lime.

Herbaceous. A non-woody plant with leaves and sometimes flowers, usually perennial. See under *Border*.

Herbal. A book which lists plants and herbs with a description of their properties. The most famous British herbals are John Gerard's *Herball or General Historie of Plants* (1597) and Nicholas Culpeper's (1652), which is still available in reprint.

Herbarium. (1) A collection of dried and preserved plants, or the building housing them. Several such collections have survived, including Philip Miller's and Sir Hans Sloane's, which both date from the eighteenth century. (2) (medieval). A small garden or, later, an arbour; cf. *Herber*.

Herber (medieval). A pleasure ground or, alternatively, an arbour.

Herb garden. A garden for the cultivation of herbs primarily for medicinal or culinary purposes (see also *Physic garden*). Subsidiary purposes included dyeing and sweetening the air in a house. A herb garden has been re-created behind Kew Palace, Surrey.

Herm. Strictly, a representation of a head of Hermes rising from a pedestal, used in classical times to mark boundaries. In gardens the word is used loosely to signify any head on a pedestal which is either rectangular or tapers downwards (cf. *Term*). Herms are often found opposite each other in rows. Chatsworth, Derbyshire, and Chiswick, Middlesex, are but two of many gardens that have groups.

Hermitage. A building generally of rustic or primitive construction which might be supposed to be the appropriate habitation for a hermit. There was a craze for them in the eighteenth century in Britain and also on the continent, and they would vary from fairly substantial (though still rustic) edifices in stone (e.g. Kent's Hermitage at Stowe, Buckinghamshire) to simple timber constructions, sometimes faced with tree trunks and thatched (e.g. Charles Hamilton's at Painshill, Surrey, or Thomas Wright's at Badminton, Avon).

Hortus conclusus (Latin = enclosed garden). A secret garden within a garden (see also *Giardino segreto*). There is a literary/religious symbolism drawn from the *Song of Songs* which associated the Virgin Mary with the term: 'enclosed' represented her intact virginity, and the flowers of virtue would grow in the garden. In practice the enclosed garden was often a rose garden with fountains, walks and arbours, surrounded by a hedge or wall, sometimes with turfed seats (q.v.), a lawn and paths. Some enclosed gardens were ecclesiastical, others secular, and their purpose was delectation and entertainment.

Hortus deliciarum (Latin = garden of delights). A term used specifically to refer to the womb of the Virgin Mary in the spiritual interpretation of hortus conclusus.

Hotbed. A bed that is hollowed out, like a trough, and filled with materials such as manure and tanner's bark which heat up and nourish the plants grown in the bed. It can be covered with a glass frame. David Garrick's poem 'The Hot-Bed's Advice to a certain Gardener' ends with the couplet :

Be quiet, Brother, wisely think,
The more we stir, the more we stink.

Hothouse. A greenhouse for the nurture of plants that need plenty of warmth. A special heating system (for example, underfloor hot-water pipes) is required.

Hunting lodge. See *Lodge*.

Hybrid. A plant that is the result of uniting two different genera, species or varieties.

Hydraulics. The science of manipulating water, primarily through pipes or fountains. The Romans used water in a sophisticated way but were eclipsed by Italian Renaissance and later French engineers. See *Automata*, *Giochi d'acqua* and *Waterworks*.

Icehouse. The first important icehouse in England was built c.1600 at Holkham Hall, Norfolk. Often recessed into the side of a hill, typical icehouses had a shaft or well, made of brick or stone, which was packed with crushed ice, sometimes salted to harden it. The entrance was lined with straw for insulation; good drainage was necessary. Icehouses were essential adjuncts to large houses in the eighteenth and nineteenth centuries for the preservation of (especially) meat and could be elaborate Gothic or classical structures such as those at Dodington House, Avon, or Penrhyn Castle, Gwynedd. The Holkham example is thatched, with a Flemish

Icehouse: Powis Castle, Powys.

Indian: bridge, Sezincote, Gloucestershire.

gabled entrance. J. C. Loudon describes and illustrates an icehouse in his *Encyclopaedia of Gardening* (1835).

Illusion. See *Perspective* and *Trompe l'oeil*.

Imp-garden (medieval). A nursery garden (imp = shoot, young tree or plant).

Improvement (mid to late eighteenth century). A term initially referring to agricultural improvement became applied to landscaping, including ornamental planting.

Improver (mid to late eighteenth century). One who 'improves' a garden by landscaping, as did Brown and Repton. The term was sometimes used satirically to suggest that the improver did not improve anything.

Incident. A garden feature (building or other construction) along the route of a garden circuit.

Indian. Characteristic of the courtly Hindu or Mogul gardens are an emphasis on richly scented plantings, trees with dark spreading

Ironwork: 'bird cage', Melbourne Hall, Derbyshire.

Italianate: Hever Castle, Kent.

foliage for shade, use of striking colour and water in a central position, often with fountains. Indian motifs were occasionally taken up in western gardens, most notably in Sezincote, Gloucestershire (early 1800s), where, apart from the Indian-style house (which inspired the Royal Pavilion at Brighton), there are a Hindu temple and pool, a bridge with Brahminee bulls on the balustrade, a serpent and an Indian conservatory.

Indoor garden. Gardens indoors have tended to consist of surrounded atrium-style areas in large public buildings. One of the most elaborate is the rockery and water garden within Sovereign House, Pimlico, London.

Informal. Design or planting without regularity or geometry.

Ionic. See *Orders of architecture*.

Iris garden. A garden, or area within a garden, in which varieties of iris are grown. As a result of hybridisation in the nineteenth and twentieth centuries, elaborate displays are now possible. Many public parks and horticultural gardens have iris beds or gardens. Kew and Wisley, both in Surrey, have iris gardens.

Ironwork. Wrought iron has for centuries been used in gardens, especially for gates. The ironwork screen at Hampton Court, Middlesex, by Tijou (c.1690) is of exceptional quality, as is the delightful 'bird-cage' arbour at Melbourne Hall, Derbyshire, by Robert Bakewell a few years later. Other types of feature, such as the pergola at Westonbirt House, Gloucestershire, are made of wrought iron. From the industrial revolution cast iron made possible the mass production of railings, posts, fountains, greenhouses, gates, urns and garden furniture.

Islamic. Islamic gardens are, or were, to be found in many areas: Spain, Turkey, North Africa, the Middle East, Asia. Although there are regional differences, there is always an emphasis on water, geometry, shade, retreat and pleasure – and an underlying religious meaning. The typical Islamic garden is divided into four quarters, separated by canals in the shape of a cross, often with a pavilion at the centre.

Island bed. A bed surrounded by grass, so that it appears to be an island in a sea of green.

Italian. Normally understood as the characteristics of an Italian garden are the features associated with the elaborate gardens of the Renaissance – formal, geometrical layouts of lawn and paths, much use of stone steps, balustrades, statuary and fountains, terraces and ingenious water effects. Some of the gardens, like Bomarzo, Lazio, Italy, had an involved allegorical scheme that cannot be readily interpreted today.

Italianate. The term can apply to the use of (particularly Renaissance) Italian features in other countries at any period, including Britain, but has special reference to the High Victorian revival of terraced gardens such as at Bowood, Wiltshire, or at Shrubland, Suffolk, which has a magnificent series of steps between the five levels.

Jacobean garden. Following the Tudor period, Jacobean gardens were still formal in layout, containing topiary, knots, herb gardens and flower parterres. Elaborate Italian Mannerist water effects and grottoes were introduced at Somerset House and Greenwich, London, and at Richmond Palace, Surrey.

Japanese. Japanese gardens have traditionally embodied deep philosophical and symbolic meanings and cannot therefore very easily transfer to the west, with its very different culture. There may be great significance in the exact placing of a rock in a plot of raked earth or gravel, or in the way in which trees are trained. The Japanese have always loved to create miniature landscapes with simple materials – a pool, an island, a bridge or stepping

*Japanese:
Newstead Abbey,
Nottinghamshire.*

stones, with cherry or other trees grown with an emphasis on line.
A Japanese-style garden has been created at Capel Manor, Middlesex.

Jardin anglais. A French term for a garden in the informally
landscaped style of the English garden. The term could embrace
both the design of the garden and the inclusion of garden buildings
in the pictorial eighteenth-century English manner.

Jardin anglo-chinois. See *Anglo-chinois*.

Jardin pittoresque (French). A type of pictorial and associative
garden found particularly in eighteenth-century France, e.g. the
Désert de Retz, influenced by artists, *fabriques* (q.v.) and the
English 'picturesque'.

Jardinet (Victorian). An ornate circular basin not for water but
for plants and shrubs, for example on a terrace.

Jardinière. A container for flowers or plants, or the ensemble of
a stand (often of ironwork) and one or more such containers.

Kennels. Ornamental kennels were popular in the later eighteenth
and early nineteenth centuries, when they appear in a number of
pattern books. The kennels at Milton Park, Cambridgeshire (1767),
resemble a ruined castle gatehouse.

Kiosk. An Islamic pavilion, open-sided or closed, found in the
Middle East from the thirteenth century. The term is applied to

small garden shelters in pictorial eighteenth-century gardens, not only of Islamic style but also Gothic or rustic. The French 'kiosque' embraced garden temples and pavilions generally. A Moorish kiosk can be seen in the nineteenth-century gardens of Linderhof, Bavaria.

Kitchen garden.   An area, often walled, for the cultivation of vegetables, fruit and herbs for culinary use. The Egyptians, Greeks and Romans grew produce in discrete garden areas for their own use and also for sale. The walled garden is commonly found in European gardens from the seventeenth century to the nineteenth. Borders adjoining the walls would be planted with fruit, often trained against the wall, and some salad species, while the beds would contain root vegetables. T. H. Mawson designed a walled kitchen garden for the first Lord Leverhulme at Thornton Manor, Wirral, Cheshire.

Knoll.   A small hill, sometimes artificial (cf. *Mount*), as they are at Kew, Surrey.

Knot garden.   A garden plot which contains intricate designs resembling knots, common in English gardens of the sixteenth and seventeenth centuries. The outline of the knot would generally be formed by a low-growing hedge of box or a line of rosemary or thyme, while the spaces would be filled with flowers, coloured earth or gravel. Knots reconstructed in the twentieth century can be seen at Hampton Court, Middlesex; Sylvia Landsberg's

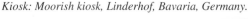

Kiosk: Moorish kiosk, Linderhof, Bavaria, Germany.

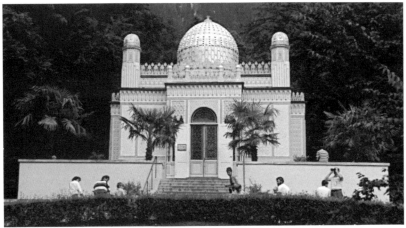

Tudor garden, Tudor House Museum, Southampton, Hampshire; and Lady Salisbury's at Hatfield House, Hertfordshire, and the Museum of Garden History, Lambeth, London. The terms 'open' and 'closed' knots are sometimes encountered, but there is confusion as to the precise significance of this distinction.

Labyrinth. An intricate pattern of paths. The idea goes back to antiquity: the hedge maze recognisable today is a development from the seventeenth century. Philip Miller described labyrinths as winding paths cut through woods or wildernesses, creating difficulty in reaching the centre. The labyrinth at the Jardin des Plantes, Paris, is a spiral path leading up to the top of a mount, planted formally with cone-shaped yews. A labyrinth cut in turf form based on the old classical design can be seen at Somerton, Oxfordshire.

Laiterie. See *Dairy*.

Lake. A prominent feature in many gardens, often artificially created or adapted. The traditional placing of a lake has been in the middle ground of a large garden, with a lawn or parterre in the foreground and a park in the background, perhaps with ornamental plantings. Lake-making could achieve great subtlety: the lake at Cirencester Park, Gloucestershire, was a very early example of one that concealed its ends, while the Broadwater at Oatlands, Surrey, was contrived to give a trompe l'oeil effect of flowing under Walton Bridge. The lake at Painshill, Surrey, has immense subtlety in not being able to be seen all at once and continually changing its shape and apparent area. 'Capability' Brown constructed many fine lakes, none more splendid than his masterpiece at Blenheim, Oxfordshire, where he saw that by damming the river Glyme and widening the water under Vanbrugh's massive bridge (and indeed flooding its lower chambers) he could create a perfect proportion of bridge and water.

Landscape garden. A garden on a large scale, naturalistic in appearance and having no regularity of design. The concept was developed from early in the eighteenth century in England and by later in the century had spread widely not only in Britain but throughout Europe. It could embrace both the pictorial, temple-clad landscape such as Painshill, Surrey, or Stourhead, Wiltshire, and the park landscapes of 'Capability' Brown and his followers (see *Brownian*). Although the appearance was natural, a great deal of art in planning and planting often lay behind it. As the term suggests, the garden becomes a landscape and indeed often brings the farmland and countryside outside to the view as well (see *Ha-ha*).

Landscape garden: Stourhead, Wiltshire.

Lawn. Philip Miller in his *Gardeners Dictionary* defined a lawn as a great plain in a park or a spacious plain adjoining a noble seat, never less than 30 to 40 acres (16 hectares) in large gardens or 8 to 10 acres (4 hectares) in modest ones. The historical lawn, therefore, is far removed from the modern small, well-trimmed suburban garden lawn. The idea of the landscape lawn was to give a sense of openness, although it was recommended that trees be planted, if possible irregularly, on the boundary for effect and for shade. Turf was preferable to sown grass. Some lawns were not of grass, for example a camomile lawn. Many impressive lawns survive, such as that stretching down from the house at Stowe, Buckinghamshire. See also *Forest lawn.*

Leadwork. Lead artefacts, particularly statuary and vases, enjoyed a particular vogue in Britain c.1680-1780. Lead figures were made from casts, so that more than one copy of the same figure could be produced, and were generally painted, either naturalistically or to look like stone or bronze. The three great masters of leadwork in this period were John Van Nost the elder, Andrew Carpenter and John Cheere. Their work can be seen in many gardens, but of special interest are the assemblages at Studley Royal, North Yorkshire; Melbourne Hall, Derbyshire; Powis Castle, Powys; and Bicton and Castle Hill, both Devon. Some of the work could reach high levels of imagination and execution, e.g. the large vase at Melbourne Hall,

Leadwork: figure of 'Painting', Anglesey Abbey, Cambridgeshire.
Maze: Woburn Abbey, Bedfordshire.

with its 'seasons' faces, monkeys and basket of fruit.

Limonaia. Lemon house, very common in Italy (cf. *Orangery*).

Linnaean system. See *Binomial system*.

Lodge. A dwelling at the entrance of an estate. The architecture of a lodge and the gate piers can be of great interest and quality and often bears a relationship to the house (e.g. the Jacobean domed roofs of the lodges at Westonbirt House, Gloucestershire, reflecting the dome of the house itself) or to some feature in the grounds to which attention is to be drawn, or it serves to establish an appropriate feeling (e.g. Repton's castellated lodge at Blaise, Bristol, which anticipates the earlier-built Blaise Castle, to be seen later in the approach). A large estate can have several lodges: there is a particularly attractive collection – five lodges and two gates – at Clumber Park, Nottinghamshire. A hunting lodge would provide a temporary stop during hunting or a viewing station for the chase, as at Chatsworth, Derbyshire.

Loggia. A covered cloister or arcade, open to the side, often attached to the house.

Mall. A shaded walk; an alley for the game of pall-mall (similar to croquet), hence the name of the London street.

Market garden. A garden in which fruit and vegetables are grown for sale.

Mary garden. A monastery garden with medicinal and culinary herbs and flowers associated symbolically with the Virgin Mary.

Massed bed. A flower bed that shows solid massing of a single species and colour. Popular in the early Victorian period, the taste followed the claim that nature masses single flowers together. Each bed, however, could contrast with its neighbour, preferably as strikingly as possible.

Massif (French). A grouping or packed cluster of trees, shrubs or other plants.

Mausoleum. A decorative tomb or building that houses a number of tombs. One of the most impressive and extensive is Hawksmoor's at Castle Howard, North Yorkshire (1730-40). A mausoleum to a single person is Robert Adam's elegant temple at Bowood, Wiltshire, for the first Marquess of Lansdowne (1761). John Donowell designed the mausoleum at West Wycombe, Buckinghamshire (1750s), for Sir Francis Dashwood, with an elaborate flint-faced screen.

Maze. The maze is a very ancient form which has appeared in many shapes and sizes, but all mazes have a deliberate design containing twists and turns. Many people use the terms 'maze' and 'labyrinth' synonymously. Early mazes were unicursal, with just one path to the centre, such as the turf maze where the shallow

Mausoleum: Castle Howard, North Yorkshire.

ditches dug to make the shape formed the barriers. There would often be a mythological or religious significance. Modern 'turf' mazes usually have paths of hard paving with turf forming the barriers, as in the Archbishop's Maze at Grey's Court, Oxfordshire. At Victoria Park, Bristol, the path is raised above water. The form with which we are most familiar today, the hedge maze, is a development (seventeenth century) of an idea that goes back to ancient Egypt and Rome (see *Labyrinth*). This sort of maze is often constructed as a puzzle, with blind alleys and curving or straight paths bounded by hedges, where the aim is to confuse the visitor, who has to try to reach the centre. The famous maze at Hampton Court, Middlesex, is probably early eighteenth-century, constructed on the site of a wilderness.

Meadow. A richly grassed area for mowing or pasture. A water meadow is adjacent to a river that may overflow.

Medieval garden. Although visual material to show what British medieval gardens looked like is lacking, we have plenty of written evidence of the great interest in gardening. There were kitchen gardens, herb gardens, the pomarium or orchard, the physic garden, the herber, the viridarium and the larger pleasance or park. Gardens were enclosed, often walled and laid out in strictly geometrical form. Queen Eleanor's Garden at Winchester Castle, Hampshire, is a modern reconstruction of a thirteenth-century garden. See also *Raised beds* and *Turfed seats*.

Melon pit or stove. See *Pit* and *Stove*.

Menagerie. A collection of wild animals or birds (see also *Aviary*), as at Woburn Abbey, Bedfordshire. In a garden context the collection did not necessarily have to be kept in cages: some animals and ornamental fowl would be allowed to roam. The Menagerie at Horton, Northamptonshire, is a building that was intended partly for animals and partly as a banqueting room.

Messuage. A term used, especially in legal documents, to indicate an estate including the house.

Military garden. A number of military architects have been involved in garden design, for example Maréchal Vauban in France. Several features are common to earthworks for military purposes and to ditches and ramparts in gardens. A military garden by name was created at Blenheim, Oxfordshire – an enormous regular structure with fortified walls of rubble and eight massive circular bastions.

Milliarium. An ornate milestone, such as was designed for Kedleston Hall, Derbyshire.

Mingling (especially nineteenth century). See *Mixed border*.

Mirador (Spanish). A prospect tower or belvedere as part of a

Menagerie: 'Menagerie House', Nostell Priory, West Yorkshire.

Spanish house, giving views of the surrounding countryside.

Mixed border or bed. A border or bed in which different species and colours are mixed; in the mid nineteenth century there was considerable friction between this principle and that of massed beds. In practice mixing tended to be in borders rather than beds.

Moat. Originally a strip of water surrounding a castle for defensive purposes, the moat from Jacobean times could be used to surround country houses purely for ornamental effect. Sometimes a moat dating back to an earlier time has subsequently been made a decorative feature, as at Hever Castle, Kent.

Monastery garden. In medieval times a number of garden areas would be cultivated around a monastery or nunnery. There would be recreational gardens with trees and walks in addition to the functional areas of orchard and kitchen garden. Herbs were grown for medicinal purposes and there was great interest in nurseries. Some monasteries created flourishing commercial enterprises out of selling seeds and plants.

Moon door. A circular opening in a door or wall. In Chinese gardens the shape may vary from circular to octagonal and to outlines of gourds or leaves. A modern example is at Hill Pasture, Essex.

Moorish. Some of the legacy of the Moors' occupation of Spain is still to be seen in Spanish gardens: elements of patio, order,

Moat: Oxburgh Hall, Norfolk.

geometry, benches, walls, evergreens and division into a number of small compartments. Water was important, and this too was 'divided' into separate pools and fountains. The Generalife gardens of Granada give some idea of the Moorish style, although much modified over the years.

Mosaïculture. A French term for a hybrid form of the English Victorian flower bed and carpet bed. From the 1860s the French (and later the Italians) devised intricate schemes where not only did the flowers create patterns and even biblical scenes, but the beds themselves were shaped like vases or birds.

Mosque. A representation of an Islamic mosque, whether for use or decoration, in a garden. They featured in the eighteenth-century landscape garden, as at Schwetzingen, Germany. Sir William Chambers designed one (now lost) at Kew, Surrey, as part of his collection of 'oriental' buildings.

Mossery. A collection of different mosses.

Moss hut (Victorian). A garden building made basically of wood in a primitive style, as at Alton Towers, Staffordshire. Branches of pine and laurel were often used, with moss pressed between the wall slats. The mosses could be of different types, thus forming a mossery. Instead of moss, heath could be used to fill in the interstices, and the exterior could be thatched with heath, making it a heath house. An example of the latter is at Drumlanrig, Dumfries

Moorish: orange tree garden, Seville cathedral, Spain.

and Galloway. A third related form was the bark house, ornamented or thatched with bark, although sometimes composed of wood with the bark still on.

Motte. A medieval mound, often forming the basis of a garden mount.

Mount. An artificial hill to provide a good view in (especially) Tudor gardens. In 1529 the mount at New College, Oxford, was made, which survives, and four years later the great mount at Hampton Court, Middlesex, was constructed, with spiralling walks and a gazebo on top. This was at the far end of the Privy Garden overlooking the Thames. Mounts could be quite large – 10 metres was a recommended size. Francis Bacon praised them in 1625, and by the early eighteenth century there was one established in Kensington Gardens, London, subsequently planted up for emphasis.

Municipal park. See *Public park*.

Museum. Literally, the haunt or home of the muses. In gardens a museum does not have to carry the modern sense of a display of scientific or other related objects: the Museum at Enville, Staffordshire (Sanderson Miller, 1750s), was also known as the Summerhouse or Billiard Room.

Nappe (French). A smooth sheet of water, either vertical (a waterfall) or horizontal (a still basin).

Natural. At various periods what was taken to be 'natural' gardening varied considerably. It is a paradox that the early eighteenth-century gardens in England could exhibit some of the 'natural' qualities extolled by writers such as Addison and Pope, while still being rigidly geometrical in layout, while equally the term 'natural gardening' in the 1870s could be applied to a revival of formally laid-out flower gardens. In the first case 'natural' meant not pruning and shaping trees (topiary), but allowing them to grow unchecked: in the second, it was a deliberate reaction against the 'parterre king', W. A. Nesfield, whose intricate beds involved the use of coloured gravels, for it was the absence of these gravels and of architectural ornament that was described as 'natural'. The most obviously natural garden in appearance was the English landscape garden, but even that was the result of highly contrived planning.

Niche: Ham House, Surrey.

Niche. An inlet in a wall or hedge to contain a piece of sculpture; a curved recess that may be large enough to house a seat. A large niche, though, is generally an alcove.

Nursery. An area for the nurture of young plants prior to permanent planting elsewhere; in the commercial sense, an area where plants are grown for sale.

Nuttery. A wood of nut-trees.

Nymphaeum (classical). A structure dedicated to the nymphs, or where they might be supposed to live. The two characteristics of the nymphaeum are: (a) the presence of water, in the form of a pool or fountain; (b) the suggestion of a grotto, even though the architecture of the chamber might be formal. There are mentions by Roman authors of classical nymphaea, while Italian Renaissance and French formal gardens revived the idea, as at the Villa Giulia, Rome.

Obelisk: Shotover, Oxfordshire.

Orangery: Margam Park, West Glamorgan.

Obelisk. A tall pillar that tapers as it rises, then angles more sharply into a point at the top. The most common form is four-sided, though Batty Langley (1740) also designed triangular, octagonal and circular models. They were well-known in ancient Rome and in Italian and French formal gardens. Small ones are used copiously at Isola Bella, Italy, and although obelisks were usually of stone they might alternatively be of topiary. In England they would normally carry a commemorative meaning, with an appropriate inscription. Their heyday was the eighteenth century. Vanbrugh built one at Castle Howard, North Yorkshire. Others are too numerous to mention but include: William Kent's at Holkham, Norfolk, and Shotover, Oxfordshire; Bramham Park, West Yorkshire; Pope's memorial obelisk to his mother at Twickenham, Middlesex (now gone). They were generally placed in prominent positions, at the junction of drives or the end of allées or vistas. They may be purely decorative, as in the round pond at Chiswick, Middlesex, and (formerly) in the pond at Claremont, Surrey.

Orangery. A house for the cultivation of oranges. Since Sir Francis Carew of Beddington, Surrey, introduced oranges from France in 1562 the practice developed of growing orange trees by keeping them warm inside the orangery during the winter months and putting them outdoors in tubs in the summer. In addition to their fruit, orange trees were valued for their appearance and scented flowers. During the eighteenth century the orangery attracted the attention of most of the leading architects of the day, and many

Orangery: Osterley Park, Middlesex.
Orangery: Mount Edgcumbe, Cornwall.

glorious examples of what must be the most handsome of functional garden buildings survive: Robert Adam's at Bowood, Wiltshire, and Kenwood, London; Sir William Chambers's at Kew, Surrey; Samuel Wyatt's at Blickling Hall, Norfolk (1782); and others such as the temple orangery at Bicton, Devon, and those at Saltram, Devon, and Mount Edgcumbe, Cornwall. Eventually the orangery gave way to the Victorian glasshouses, which permitted far more heat and light to enter through the transparent roof.

Orchard. An area for the cultivation of fruit trees. However, the derivation of the word, from the Latin *hortus* (*ortus* in medieval Latin), i.e. garden, and possibly the Old English *ort-geard*, or *wort-geard*, meaning a yard for roots (= vegetables), shows that it was not originally specifically for the growing of fruit. Medieval Latin tended to use 'pomarium' for orchard, even though the word literally applies just to apples.

Orchard house. A glass forcing house for various kinds of fruit, introduced in the early nineteenth century, as at Luton Hoo, Bedfordshire. Lean-to houses were used for wall-grown fruit such as grapes and peaches, while large free-standing houses contained fruit growing in pots or on trees planted in the ground.

Orchid house. A glasshouse for the cultivation of orchids, which generally require much warmth and moisture. Until 1800 orchids were hardly known in England. Then an explosion of interest and plant-hunting secured thousands of species by the end of the century, a process accelerated by hybridisation from 1856. There were great personal collections such as R. S. Holford's at Westonbirt, Gloucestershire (Victorian), while the major botanic gardens all have significant displays. Orchid houses, though generically one of a range of greenhouses and hothouses, are dedicated to the plants they contain, preserving the right tropical conditions of humidity and temperature.

Orders of architecture. For a full description of the orders of classical architecture, and other architectural terms, the reader is referred to specialist dictionaries. However, the terms Doric, Ionic, Corinthian and Tuscan are frequently used in relation to classical-style garden buildings and will be briefly explained here. The orders are differentiated (a) by their columns – base, shaft and capital – and (b) by the entablature above – frieze, architrave and cornice. Reduced to its simplest, Doric has a plain (Roman) or fluted (Greek or Roman) shaft and triglyphs (patterns of three upright bars and grooves) alternating with metopes (panels, plain or decorated) in the frieze. Ionic is characterised by volutes (double

CLASSICAL COLUMNS

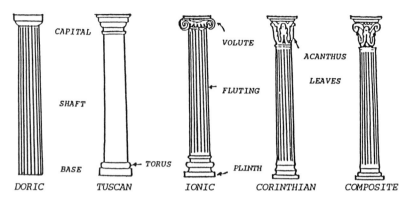

ENTABLATURE: *horizontal block supported by columns as above*

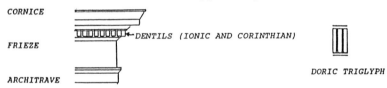

Orders of architecture.

scroll) in the capital and dentils ('teeth' with gaps) in the cornice. Corinthian normally has a fluted shaft and is distinguished by the elaborate capital decorated with acanthus or other leaves. The Tuscan (Roman) is a massive, plain style, a form of Doric, with no decoration in the entablature and a single torus (convex rim) base where the other orders have two; or (as with the Tuscan Temple at Rievaulx Terrace, North Yorkshire) no base at all.

Overthrow. The decorative wrought ironwork surmounting an iron gate.

Pagoda. The most popular of Chinese (or chinoiserie) garden houses. Tall, usually tapering, slender and with several storeys, the pagoda lends itself well to chinoiserie decoration, having so many corner angles. For example, Sir William Chambers's pagoda at Kew, Surrey, the best-known of the genre, formerly had a dragon finial at each corner, before the Prince Regent, in one of his periodic spells of impecunity, sold them off. There were many pagodas in eighteenth-century English gardens (e.g. Marybone, Gloucestershire), and the idea lingered on into the nineteenth century – the iron pagoda at Alton Towers, Staffordshire (1828). The pagoda at Woburn Abbey, Bedfordshire, dates from 1833 but was taken from a Chambers design of 1757.

Pale. A wooden stake driven into the ground for fencing; hence, paling = fence.

Palisade. A fence of stakes or pales.

Palissade (French). A hedge clipped to form an even wall.

Palladian bridge. See *Bridge*.

Palm house. A glasshouse for the cultivation of palm trees and other tropical plants. The enormous progress in technology in Victorian times embraced both the use of cast iron and glass on an extensive scale and improvements in heating. These together enabled species such as palms, which required a large space and also considerable heat and moisture, to be grown indoors. The most famous in England is the Palm House at Kew, Surrey (Decimus Burton and Richard Turner, 1848). Another is at Bicton, Devon.

Paradeisos (Greek, of Persian origin). An extensive enclosure, filled with wild animals. There would be a hunting park and also areas for fruit, trees, flowers and recreation.

Park. An enclosed piece of land, generally large in area. The essence of the medieval park was that it was an area for hunting; much would be covered with woodland, through which broad rides were cut. The process of enclosing land for timber cultivation and hunting was known as emparking. In the eighteenth century the concept of the park developed as an area planned for visual enjoyment, naturalistic in appearance, with rolling downs, careful location of trees, often a lake, and maintained by those cheapest of gardeners, deer and sheep. 'Capability' Brown's name is closely associated with this concept of the park (see *Brownian*). A more specialised use of the word is found in Scotland, where it can refer to enclosed farm-ground or a field. See also *Royal parks* and *Public parks*.

Parterre. A flat terrace usually adjacent or near to the house and laid out with flower beds or other decorative patterns in regular formation, to be seen from above. A parterre in England could be entirely plain, simply turf with walks alongside. Philip Miller recommended oblong as a good shape for a parterre. A grand parterre of the seventeenth century, but much elaborated in 1830, can be seen at Drummond Castle, Tayside.

Parterre à l'anglaise (French = parterre in the English manner). This parterre is basically a turfed lawn and the design is cut into

Overthrow: the Norfolk Gates, Sandringham, Norfolk.
Palm house: Belfast Botanic Gardens, Northern Ireland.

Pagoda: Kew Gardens, Surrey.

the turf. See also *Plat*.

Parterre de broderie (French = embroidered parterre). This fashion was popularised by Mollet in seventeenth-century France. It consisted of foliage patterns created by the use of box bordering a bed of coloured earth, sometimes with bands of turf. An example designed by Le Notre was at Fontainebleau (1645). Parterres de broderie spread to some extent elsewhere in Europe but fell out of fashion by the end of the eighteenth century. They enjoyed a

Parterre: Edzell Castle, Tayside.

Patio: Generalife, Granada, Spain.

Patte d'oie: Chiswick House, Middlesex (engraving, 1753).

Victorian revival in Britain, however, especially under W. A. Nesfield, e.g. at Eaton Hall, Cheshire.

Parterre de compartiment (French). An embroidered parterre symmetrical about both vertical and horizontal axes.

Pasture. Land used for grazing by cattle.

Patio (Spanish = courtyard). The superb gardens of the Generalife, Granada, Spain, have a number of patios containing pools, basins or fountains. In Britain today the term is commonly applied to a small paved area adjacent to a house where chairs and tables can be set.

Patte d'oie (French = goose foot). A feature common in French formal gardens, where several straight allées radiate forwards from a single point (usually the house). The idea may have come from Italian town planning: Palladio's designs for streets in Vicenza show such a pattern. In England two notable examples are to be found in Lord Burlington's Italianate garden at Chiswick, Middlesex (from 1715), while others survive at Inkpen Old Rectory, Berkshire (1695), St Paul's Walden Bury, Hertfordshire (c.1725), and Bramham, West Yorkshire (1700-30), all of which were influenced by French layouts.

Pattern book (eighteenth/nineteenth century). A book of designs for buildings and other garden furnishings.

Pavilion. A garden building, often light, airy and open; or containing one or more rooms. The term comes from the large tents of the Middle and Far East. Initially, in English gardens of the sixteenth century, a pavilion was always a tent of canvas. Some pavilions could actually be lived in: the Royal Pavilion at Brighton, East Sussex (completed 1822), is hardly a garden building, but it shows that the word could be applied to a whole suite of rooms. Thomas Archer's pavilion at Wrest Park, Bedfordshire (1712), has rooms in the roof as well as on the main floor and downstairs. The Oval Pavilion at Farnborough Hall, Warwickshire, has an exquisite tiny rococo room above a seat. A semicircle of supper boxes at Vauxhall Gardens, London, was described c.1750 as the 'Chinese pavillions'.

Paving. Cut stone, brick or tile for walking on. Other materials are wood and concrete.

Peat garden. A garden founded on peat. To prevent any adverse reaction with lime soil, peat beds are often raised and laid against a wall. The wall itself is sometimes of peat blocks. Woodland plants and heathers do particularly well in peat.

Pebblework. The use of pebbles to form designs on a wall or to act as flooring for a garden structure. Kent's pebble alcove at

Pavilion: Wrest Park, Bedfordshire.   *Pebblework: Stowe, Buckinghamshire.*

Stowe, Buckinghamshire, picks out the Temple family arms in coloured stones, which are also used to create a geometrical pattern. Many examples exist of pebbles paving the floor of grottoes (e.g. Stourhead, Wiltshire).

Pedestal. A block on which an urn or figure stands, for enhanced display. It may be decorative in its own right, as Hawksmoor's attractively embellished pedestals for the statuary at Castle Howard, North Yorkshire, or the Roman pedestal supporting an eighteenth-century vase with Bacchic frieze at Anglesey Abbey, Cambridgeshire.

Pelouse (French). A sweeping lawn in a landscape garden.

Percée (French). A walk cut through a wood.

Pergola. A structure of uprights and connecting joists or arches for supporting climbing plants or fruit trees. It can often give an 'arched tunnel' effect (cf. *Tunnel-arbour*). In the sixteenth century the term referred to a balcony. A pergola over 90 metres long by Peto is at West Dean, West Sussex.

Peristyle garden. A Roman courtyard garden surrounded by the house or a colonnade (see also *Viridiarium*).

Perspective. (1) (seventeenth century) A painting of a trompe l'oeil kind in oil or fresco covering a wall at the end of an allée. (2) (general) Perspective plays an important part in many garden views. Just as an artist or theatrical scene-painter can create and manipulate perspective, so a garden designer can arrange objects or plantings to bring focal points nearer or to distance them. Alexander Pope spoke of the technique used in his own garden: 'You may distance things by darkening them, and by narrowing the plantation more and more towards the end, in the same manner as they do in painting, and as 'tis executed in the little cypress walk to that obelisk.' The series of triumphal arches at Vauxhall Gardens, London, was composed in a theatrical way to heighten the perspective of one of the walks.

Pheasantry. A cage to keep and display pheasants, bred for their ornamental appearance. Sometimes the buildings themselves would be ornamental, with designers such as Humphry Repton. Sir William Chambers designed the pheasantry at Kew, Surrey, c.1758 (also known as the pheasant ground). Another was built at Haddo House, Grampian Region, in 1885.

Physic garden. A garden with medicinal plants. Historically the physic garden was concerned with the development of botany and had much in common with the botanic garden. But the term 'physic' (= healing) became attached specifically to the cultivation of herbs with medicinal properties (cf. *Herb garden*). The Chelsea

Pergola: Westonbirt House, Gloucestershire.
Pineapple, pine cone: Chiswick House, Middlesex.

Physic Garden, London, was founded in 1673 and is still concerned with research and the study of plants.

Picturesque. The Picturesque was a movement which reached its height towards the end of the eighteenth century. After William Gilpin (who first used the word in 1748) popularised the wild scenery of the Wye Valley and the Lake District from the mid century onwards, two Herefordshire squires, Richard Payne Knight and Sir Uvedale Price, sought to define the Picturesque as a particular type of scenery that was suitable for painting – broken, irregular, varied and often spectacular. (For contrast, see *Beautiful*.) Both men were firmly anti-Brown, whose work they found insipid and dull. In gardens the Picturesque approach is characterised by use of dramatic scenery (where it exists), contrasts of texture and vegetation, and a sense of wildness in that bushes, shrubs and trees are allowed to proliferate without apparent check, to give a shaggy or overgrown effect to the view. Picturesque gardens include Mount Edgcumbe, Cornwall; Wardour and Fonthill, both Wiltshire; and Payne Knight's and Price's own estates at Downton and Foxley, Herefordshire. Humphry Repton devised a rather cosier version, a sort of villa picturesque with flower gardens near the house. His larger landscapes were concerned with massing or thinning trees to optimise the view and to display the house in its best setting (see also *Approach* and *Drive*). Shrubberies in Regency gardens (q.v.) were also described as picturesque.

Pièce d'eau (French). A formal pond or basin, generally of stone.

Pier. See *Gate pier*.

Pigeon house. See *Dovecote*.

Pineapple, pine cone. Ornamental finial. A small pine cone can serve as a decoration on, for example, an urn (see illustration).

Pinepit. A pit or hotbed (q.v.) for growing pineapples.

Pinery. A greenhouse for the cultivation of pineapples; or a wood of pine-trees.

Pinetum. A collection of trees (cf. *Arboretum*) composed of conifers. The best example is Bedgebury Pinetum, Kent, but there are sometimes smaller-scale pineta within varied gardens.

Pit. A trough or sunken bed which was kept warm or hot for the cultivation of tropical species, such as melon and pineapple. See *Hotbed*.

Plant hunters. Plants have been sought and brought back from foreign parts since antiquity. It is not, however, until the seventeenth century (in Britain) that the name can properly be applied to those who voyaged far and often dangerously to seek out new and exciting plants. The Tradescants, father and son, travelled to Russia,

Pit: Calke Abbey, Derbyshire.

Plate-bande: Het Loo, Netherlands.

Morocco and Virginia, USA, during the seventeenth century, to begin a movement that gathered momentum through the eighteenth century, particularly with regard to plants from North America (many from the Bartrams in Pennsylvania). Towards the end of that century the South Seas were explored, and in the nineteenth century came the golden age of expeditions to the Himalayas (by Hooker and others) and to the East to bring back specimens for the benefit of Kew especially.

Planter. A decorative container for growing plants. It can be, for example, attached to a wall.

Plat. A flat area (cf. *Parterre*) of plain grass, perhaps with a statue in the centre. Philip Miller recommended turf rather than sown grass for lawns and plats. Plats have been restored at Ham House, Surrey.

Plate-bande (French). The border of a parterre de broderie (q.v.). They figure in several of Mollet's seventeenth-century designs for gardens in France and the Netherlands and consist either of a strip edged with box, containing flowers, or a double strip, one containing flowers or grass and the other sand. The restored parterres at Het Loo have double plate-bandes.

Platoons. Regular clumps of trees forming an avenue, as at Bushy Park, Middlesex. Platoons of nine trees are grouped at Croxdale Hall, County Durham.

Pleaching. The practice of intertwining branches of a line of trees to create the effect of a 'hedge on stilts' (cf. *Palissade*, where the hedge generally comes down to the ground). Limes are often used, as in the pleached walk at Hall Barn, Buckinghamshire.

Pleasance (medieval). An area used for pleasure and recreation – hunting, watching rural pastimes, enjoying the ornamental plantings.

Pleasure garden. (1) A general term for pleasure ground. (2) A term specific to the private gardens, nearly all in London, which were run as commercial enterprises c.1660-1850, with particular success in the eighteenth century. The three most famous were Vauxhall, Ranelagh and Marylebone. The gardens were a meeting place for a broad spectrum of society, where people could eat, drink, promenade, listen to music, take part in masquerades and watch popular entertainments such as juggling and tightrope walking. There were firework displays such as the 'Forge of Vulcan', followed by the eruption of Mount Etna, at Marylebone. The garden layouts tended to be simple and formal, with straight walks and regular rows of trees, with some trees more thickly grown in fenced-off compartments at Vauxhall. The architecture, however, was of more interest: at Vauxhall, there were wooden triumphal arches, like the wings in a theatre, to heighten perspective; the Turkish Tent (which was more Gothic-Turkish); the row of Chinese supper boxes (which were Gothic-Chinese). At Ranelagh there was the Rotunda, 50 metres across, and, again a hybrid, the Chinese house, which was an open structure decorated with Venetian masks.

Pleasure ground (term common in the eighteenth century). An area particularly cultivated with lawns, ornamental plantings and architecture; often as opposed to the less intensively planned and maintained park. A large estate might well be divided into the two, with the pleasure grounds intended for traversing on foot, while the park would be enjoyed from horseback or horse-drawn transport.

Policies (Scottish). The ornamental grounds surrounding a large country house.

Polish hut. See under *Bengal cottage*.

Pollard. A tree that has the entire top (poll = head) cut off at a height 2-3 metres from the ground. The result is that new stems grow up and out of the top of the remaining trunk, out of the reach of browsing animals. This system of woodland management was widely practised, and many ancient pollards may still be seen today. See also *Coppice* and *Shred*.

Pomarium (medieval). An orchard.

Pommel. A finial in the shape of a ball (smooth or faceted), common on gates and walls.

Pond. A small lake or pool, often artificial.

Pool. A small area of water; in gardens either natural or artificial.

Potager (French). A kitchen or vegetable garden.

Praeneste (Roman town = modern Palestrina). An arcade in classical style formed against a hill, as at Praeneste. The name was applied to William Kent's arcade at Rousham, Oxfordshire. A similar construction, though not described as such, is at Belsay, Northumberland.

Pratum (Latin = meadow). Term used in medieval times to denote a grass area planted with trees and containing walks.

Préau (French). A square grass enclosure inside a castle or monastery.

Privy garden. A private garden for the prime or sole use of, for example, the monarch. A well-known example is at Hampton Court, Middlesex.

Promenade. An area available to the public for walking.

Prospect. A wide, panoramic view, as opposed to the narrow, framed view of a vista (q.v.).

Prospect tower. See *Tower*.

Public park. Although the royal parks had been open to the public by grace and favour for centuries, the concept of the purpose-designed public park dates only from the nineteenth century. These areas, for public recreation and totally accessible, seen as an instrument for social reform, were first developed in the first decade of Queen Victoria's reign: Liverpool (1842), Birkenhead (1844) and three in Manchester and Salford (1846). The pioneering designers included J. C. Loudon and Sir Joseph Paxton. Victoria Park and Battersea Park in London were formed while still Crown property, but with the idea of being entirely for the public, and they ceased to be Crown land in 1887. Regent's Park, London, was planned as a smart villa estate for the Prince Regent but with space for amenities for sport and recreation which became more and more publicly orientated. Most public parks today are run by the local authority and can cater for sport and leisure while at the same time often containing displays of flowers and ornamental trees.

Puddled clay. A material often used for lining the bed of an artificial lake. Clay is kneaded (puddled), sometimes with sand, to create a watertight lining.

Pulhamite (rock). A composition stone created by James Pulham and developed from the 1840s. It was formed by pouring cement on a clinker base and could realistically resemble geological strata. The rockeries at Battersea Park, London, are a well-known example of the many Pulham commissions, though now painted to look like concrete.

Pyramid. (1) A structure in brick or stone rising symmetrically from a square base to a single point at the apex. In gardens they have often been used for tombs, as at Blickling Hall, Norfolk (Joseph Bonomi, 1797). Vanbrugh built one at Stowe, Buckinghamshire, and two survive at Castle Howard, North Yorkshire.

(2) A pyramidal structure of topiary or plants trained on a rubble cone, the latter in the Victorian period. Yews were clipped into pyramids in the great fountain garden at Hampton Court, Middlesex, early in the eighteenth century. A pelargonium pyramid is depicted in an engraving of 1866, designed by Shirley Hibberd.

Quarry garden. A garden made in a quarry where the precipitous sides are used for spectacular effect, as at Belsay, Northumberland.

Quarter. A compartment of a garden, bordered by a hedge or other delineator. Until the seventeenth century it represented one quarter of a square or rectangular parterre laid out in formal French or Italian style, but later it came to be simply a compartment within a larger area, not necessarily one fourth of the whole. Wildernesses or bosquets could be divided into quarters, each with trees, shrubs or tall plants growing within the hedge border, either regularly or informally. If a quarter was large, there could be walks within it, of soil or grass. Philip Miller recommended that, although plantings could be mixed in a quarter, evergreens should not be planted with deciduous species, and the planting should be tiered with large trees in the middle and shrubs and flowers at the front.

Quincunx. A figure of trees planted in a formation resembling the five spots on a die, four at the corners of a square and one in the middle. The pattern can be repeated to form a regular grove or wilderness. A variation, once common in France, is to join the squares together so that the right corners of the first square form the left corners of the second, thus:

```
      *        *        *        *
          *        *        *
      *        *        *        *
```

A quincunx consisting of small trees and clipped evergreens is to be found surrounding the parterre of the Dutch-style garden at Westbury Court, Gloucestershire (recreated in the 1970s).

Rabbit warren. From Roman times warrens were artificially constructed for a programme of breeding and control of rabbits. A warren could form a distinct feature of a garden, such as the

Pyramid: Castle Howard, North Yorkshire.   *Rill: Rousham, Oxfordshire.*

Pond: Eagle Pond, Newstead Abbey, Nottinghamshire.

enclosed area centred by a Chinese summerhouse at the Duke of Argyll's nursery garden at Whitton, Middlesex (mid eighteenth century).

Raised bed. A bed raised, as the name suggests, above the level of the surrounding walks. Common in medieval and Renaissance enclosed gardens, the raised bed would contain flowers and plants and have a hedge or paling on one or more sides. It would be regular in shape (square or rectangular) and the slight extra height would allow drainage from the roots in wet northern European climes.

Red Book. Humphry Repton (1752-1818) devised a method of presenting his plans to a client by means of a Red Book, a hand-prepared folio of a series of watercolours with accompanying text showing views of the present state of the grounds and how they would look after his proposed improvements. This was achieved by a 'slide', a flap which could be lifted to reveal the improvement. They became known as Red Books because many (not all) were bound in red Morocco leather. They are now very scarce and jealously kept by their owners but a collection of more than forty was assembled for the exhibition on Repton at the Victoria and Albert Museum in 1982-3.

Regency garden. A prominent characteristic of the gardens of early nineteenth-century England was an emphasis on shrubberies, sometimes in island beds and sometimes acting as boundaries between one area and another. The shrubberies would be colourful and grow lavishly, with a mixture of hedgerow planting and flowers. In *Mansfield Park* Jane Austen describes a hedgerow converted into a shrubbery. The Regency garden for the Royal Pavilion at Brighton, East Sussex, is being restored, with beds that push into the lawn, serpentine paths and undulations of ground. See *Forest lawn* for the origins of this sort of design.

Reposoir. An ornamental arch with some depth to it. Repton designed a Gothic reposoir for Lady Salusbury at Bransbury (= Brondesbury, Middlesex), with an ogee arch; and the Needle's Eye, an arch cut through a pyramid at Wentworth Woodhouse, South Yorkshire, has also been so described.

Reserve (1). A tree grown (in osier cases or baskets: London and Wise, 1710) as a potential replacement for those planted in a display area in case of the loss of any of the latter.
(2) A garden plot where plants are grown for later removal to areas of display (cf. *Bedding out*).

Riad (North Africa). Garden circumscribed by colonnaded walk (cf. *Peristyle*).

Ribbon border. See *Border*.

Ride. An avenue, generally cut through a wood, for riding on horseback, for example the Ten Rides at Cirencester Park, Gloucestershire, which meet at the rondpoint (q.v.)

Riding. A drive, path or road intended originally for travel on horseback (or by horse-drawn vehicle) in the outer reaches of an estate or outside it. As Thomas Whately in his *Observations on Modern Gardening* (1770) explains, the purpose is 'to extend the idea of a seat', and to bring the decoration of a garden – trees, shrubs, underplanting – to line the road or to colour the views from it, in other words to treat the road as if it were a path within pleasure grounds.

Rill. A small stream or brook. A famous deliberately contrived example is the serpentine rill at Rousham, Oxfordshire, where a barely perceptible gradient causes the water to flow in and out of the cold bath.

River. Rivers have often formed a key feature in a garden, though they have sometimes had to be shaped and diverted to meet the designer's requirements. The river Skell at Studley Royal, North Yorkshire, is formed as a canal as it passes the Moon Ponds but emerges in more natural form as it proceeds to Fountains Abbey.

Rocaille. Rockwork, pebblework or shellwork.

Rockery. A small area with soil and pieces of rock for growing rock plants.

Rock garden. The concept of the rock garden as part of a garden where certain types of plant can be grown (cf. *Alpine garden*) is Victorian, though perhaps an extension of the grotto idea. As alpine and rock-loving plants were introduced from mountainous parts abroad, there grew a taste, which is still prevalent, for setting rocks in an area, sometimes with water, and planting the appropriate flowers and shrubs. Ferns have always featured prominently in rock gardens, and dwarf conifers have become popular in modern times. Rock gardens were given a boost by the introduction in 1848 of Pulhamite (q.v.) stone. As well as rock, related materials, e.g. scree stones, can be utilised. Famous rock gardens are at Wisley, Surrey, and the Royal Botanic Garden, Edinburgh.

Rockwork. Particularly in the eighteenth century, rockwork was used in the making of grottoes, cascades and other constructions of a rococo kind. It has been claimed that the idea of assembling rocks to create craggy arches came from China, but Chinese influence on the English garden has been disputed (see also *Anglo-chinois*). From 1750 onwards rockwork was used in a progressively naturalistic way, from the grotto at Claremont, Surrey, to the

Rococo: rococo valley, Bowood, Wiltshire.

cascade at West Wycombe, Buckinghamshire, and later to the sarsen grotto at Wardour, Wiltshire. Rocks were frequently imported from distant parts of the country, involving great expense and labour.

Rococo (from the French, rocaille = pebblework or rockwork and coquille = shell). A style characterised in the visual arts by playfulness, elegance, asymmetry and sometimes wilfulness. In English gardens the term may be applied to some smaller gardens of the mid eighteenth century, together with some individual buildings or other features in a larger garden, to demonstrate a light-hearted and fanciful approach which may take advantage of a number of different architectural styles – Gothic, Chinese, rustic. Rococo gardens include Painswick, Gloucestershire, which has some very quirky architecture and irregularity of path layout (see *Serpentine*); Hampton Court House, Middlesex, with a heart-shaped lake, icehouse, fountain arch, exedra and superb shell grotto all within a small compass; and Belcombe Court, Wiltshire, again with several features, including a grotto, close together so they can be comprehended in a single view. Rocks and shells often play a part, as for example in the 'rococo valley' at Bowood, Wiltshire, where a naturalistic waterfall covers a warren of passages, while two grotto tunnels line the cascade and the valley, and a Hermit's Cell has ammonites in the ceiling.

In German gardens the term 'rococo' has been applied to a

garden with a series of small garden rooms in a usually formal plan but containing rococo constructions – chinoiserie, ruins, grotesque figures and so on.

Roman. Classical Roman gardens were of varied kinds, as we can tell from archaeology, from remains and from descriptions: the enclosed peristyle garden (q.v.), the sacred garden (e.g. the Canopus at Hadrian's Villa, Tivoli, dedicated to the god Serapis), and large open areas where wild woods and pavilions and artificial trelliswork would be combined. Statuary featured prominently, as did plants and water (see also *Nymphaeum*).

Rondpoint. A large circular area which acts as the meeting point for a number of avenues or rides. A good example is at Cirencester Park, Gloucestershire, where ten rides meet at the rondpoint.

Roof garden. Although known in the Renaissance, roof gardens are thought of as a twentieth-century development, made possible through advances in waterproofing and construction methods. Several eminent architects – Le Corbusier, Lloyd Wright, Burle Marx, Geoffrey Jellicoe – have devoted attention to this form. In Britain, well-known examples have been sited above Derry &

Rotunda: Duncombe Park, North Yorkshire.

Toms in Kensington High Street, London (1930s), and above Harvey's at Guildford, Surrey (1956). Many roof gardens are to be found in the United States of America, Canada, Germany and Switzerland.

Room. An open space or clearing in a garden; a compartment. The 'walls' of the room may consist of fencing or hedges.

Root house. A garden building composed of, or decorated with, roots and other parts of trees – stumps, trunks, branches. Most popular in the eighteenth and nineteenth centuries, rootwork could extend to a number of structures – seats, bridges, arbours. Thomas Wright designed a number of root houses in the mid eighteenth century: one survives at Badminton, Avon, known as the Hermit's Cell, where all the furniture is also of wood, down to the loaf of bread on the table. Another example is at Spetchley Park, Worcestershire.

Roots. Perennial plants; or vegetables.

Rosarium, rosary. A rose or flower garden of a formal kind, often a circular area bounded by arches of trelliswork upon which some of the roses can be trained. Thomas Wright used the term 'rosary' for large circular flower beds mathematically composed, without particular reference to roses. Humphry Repton designed a number, including an arch-encircled one at Ashridge, Hertfordshire, but the Victorian era was their heyday. A good reconstructed example is at Warwick Castle, Warwickshire, and there is also one at Blenheim, Oxfordshire.

Rose garden. A garden or area for growing roses. In many cases the gardens continue to be geometrical in layout, as they were traditionally (see *Rosarium*), but from the time of the cottage garden (q.v.) roses have also been grown in informal manner. Displays may use many kinds of rose, which is one of the oldest-known garden flowers and which through hybridisation can assume an astonishing range of size, form and colour. From a choice of a multitude of collections, old roses can be seen at Sissinghurst Castle, Kent.

Rotunda, rotundo. A building, circular in plan, usually in the form of a dome capping a circle of columns. This is the simple basic form, open without any structure inside, although the term can also be applied to a circular temple with colonnade and interior chamber. Open rotundas are common, good examples being Vanbrugh's at Stowe, Buckinghamshire, and at Duncombe Park, North Yorkshire; Campbell's Temple of Venus at Hall Barn, Buckinghamshire; the Temple of Aeolus at Kew, Surrey; and 'Mrs Busby's Temple' at Halswell, Somerset. The closed or filled

Ruins: ruined chapel, the Leasowes, West Midlands (engraving, c.1770).

rotundas were generally modelled on the Temple of Vesta at Tivoli
and Bramante's Renaissance Tempietto, Montorio, Rome: examples are William Kent's Temple of Ancient Virtue at Stowe, Buckinghamshire; Bramham, West Yorkshire; the Mausoleum at Castle Howard, North Yorkshire, and Robert Adam's temple at Audley
End, Essex.

Royal gardens. A term used to cover the gardens of the monarch's
current residences; also those which in the past have been laid
out under royal ownership and direction but which may now be
open to the public (some of which are listed under royal parks)
or those which are or were laid out by members of the royal
family other than the monarch.

Royal park. The property of the monarch, the royal parks of London
are now all open to the public and indeed have mostly been for
centuries. Some retain signs of their original French layout –
Greenwich, St James's Park, Hampton Court – with the patte
d'oie prominent at the last. The others are Bushy Park, Richmond
Park, Kensington Gardens, Hyde Park, Green Park and Regent's
Park. Royal parks were originally large tracts of wooded country
for the purpose of hunting.

Ruins. Ruins, whether real or purpose-built, have featured in many
gardens both in Britain and abroad. The Cistercian ruins in North
Yorkshire – Rievaulx Abbey and Fountains Abbey – were focal
points of, respectively, the terrace walk above Rievaulx and the

vista from Studley Royal. These doubtless inspired other designers, who were not so fortunate as to have a real ruin, to construct
their own. Classical ruins, such as Chambers's ruined arch at
Kew, Surrey, Hamilton's Mausoleum at Painshill, Surrey, and
Thomas Wright's fragments at Shugborough, Staffordshire, would
evoke the world of the classical campagna painters such as Claude
and Poussin and also remind the viewer of the passing of time
and the decay of all things, however glorious. Gothic ruins (in
particular castles, the speciality of Sanderson Miller) would look
back to an imagined family past, redolent of medieval struggles
and great victories. Ecclesiastical ruins – chapels such as
Southcote's at Woburn Farm, Surrey, and that at Mount Edgcumbe,
Cornwall; abbeys such as that at Painshill, Surrey; priories such
as Shenstone's at the Leasowes, West Midlands – would also
have associations with the past, perhaps nostalgic as well as of
evanescence. Arthur Young wrote in 1771 of the imaginative re-
sponse to a ruin (preferably a real one): that there was a kind of
religious melancholy created by derelict and neglected ruins. He
considered that ruins were best seen at a distance, to leave a
certain amount to the imagination. In Europe ruins were also used

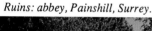

Ruins: abbey, Painshill, Surrey.

Rustic: summerhouse, Hadspen, Somerset.

for associative and sometimes philosophical purposes. The ruined Temple of Philosophy at Ermenonville indicated the incomplete and disjointed state of human thought, while the colossal ruined column at the Désert de Retz, used as the house, conveyed the vastness of the works of ancient civilisations.

Rural gardening (early eighteenth century). A term associated with extensive or forest gardening (q.v.) by Stephen Switzer, the idea being to bring the countryside into the compass of the garden (at a period of still largely formal garden design) and to consider the estate as a whole.

Russian hut. See under *Bengal cottage*.

Rustic. A style of constructing seats, buildings, etc, from simple natural materials in a crude and primitive form: thus, a hermitage in a garden might give the impression that it had been built by the hermit himself using only materials to hand. Accordingly bark, tree trunks and branches, thatch, roots and reeds were all employed. There were designs for rustic structures in the pattern books of the eighteenth and nineteenth centuries, like those by Thomas Wright, who had a special penchant for the genre, and William Wrighte. A building at Killerton, Devon, has a room with a floor of halved tree-trunks, while at Bicton in the same county the floor of the hermitage is inlaid with deer bones. There are many rustic garden houses in Scotland, e.g. the summerhouse with brown and white moss patterns and larch rod seating at Drumlanrig, Dumfries and Galloway.

Sarcophagus: Cliveden, Buckinghamshire.

Sculpture garden: Yorkshire Sculpture Park, West Yorkshire.

Rustication. A particular finish applied to masonry, often in the form of bands of frostwork or vermiculation (q.v.) on a column or pilaster.

Salle de verdure (French). A central area within a bosquet.

Sand path. Paths composed of sand were common in seventeenth- and early eighteenth-century gardens.

Sarcophagus. Sometimes used as an ornament in a garden among other classical remains, as at Iford Manor, Wiltshire.

Saut de loup (French = wolf's jump). A ditch dug at the end of an allée which is not seen but which prevents animals encroaching (cf. *Ha-ha*).

Scots cottage. See under *Bengal cottage*.

Scree garden. See *Rock garden*.

Screen. (1) A protective row of trees.

(2) An ornamental frame of wrought ironwork, such as Tijou's at Hampton Court, Middlesex. Shirley Hibberd (1875) describes what is referred to as an 'elephant trap', a flat screen with perspective fencing and path on it to mask a road behind.

Sculpture. See *Statuary*.

Sculpture garden. A garden, private or public, where sculpture is displayed. The 'purest' form of the sculpture garden is where the garden and the sculpture have both been designed together as an integral concept. These are commonest in some twentieth-century gardens in America and Scandinavia. More usual, however, is a pre-existing garden where sculpture is placed. Many public sculpture parks have been created in recent times, such as the Yorkshire Sculpture Park, Wakefield, West Yorkshire, which has special exhibition displays, for example the *Family of Man* by Barbara Hepworth, who, along with Elisabeth Frink and Henry Moore, was long interested in the unity and relationship between man and nature and between sculpture and its setting. Classical Roman gardens were often sculpture gardens by virtue of the number of figures they contained, as indeed were many traditional Italian and French gardens.

Seat. (1) A mansion or family home. The term is used particularly in the seventeenth to nineteenth centuries.

(2) A garden chair or bench with a back. It may be of a variety of materials, commonly wood, stone or cast iron. In the eighteenth and nineteenth centuries seats were taken seriously as works of art and exhibited a number of design styles, just as interior furniture would. In the eighteenth-century pattern books (as indeed in practice) there are some astonishing designs for Chinese and rustic seats.

(3) A term for a seat and its shelter together (cf. *Alcove*). William Kent designed an elegant trelliswork pair at Rousham, Oxfordshire, and another by or after him is also to be seen at Euston Hall, Suffolk.

(4) A shelter without a seat, although one may have existed at some time. The Gothic Seat at Painswick, Gloucestershire, does not have one.

Secret garden. See *Giardino segreto.*

Sedilia. Bench-type seat in a niche in a wall, as at Gunnersbury Park, London.

Serpentine. The serpentine shape is associated with Hogarth's 'waving line of beauty' in the 1750s, but

Seat: Euston Hall, Suffolk.

serpentine paths in wildernesses were widely used by the end of the seventeenth century, in much more convoluted form than Hogarth's more gentle curve. In the early eighteenth century Stephen Switzer and Batty Langley drew designs for serpentine paths in their text books, and Switzer probably designed the labyrinthine paths in Wray Wood at Castle Howard, North Yorkshire. The serpentising of water was also known from the late seventeenth century and was given recognition by the name of the first lake in such shape, the Serpentine in London's Kensington Gardens (1731). Also in the 1730s William Kent designed the serpentine rill at Rousham, Oxfordshire. Winding forms were taken up a little later in a rococo context, for example by the patte d'oie at Painswick, Gloucestershire, where two paths are straight, as they should traditionally be, and the third wiggles about; or by the water at Wroxton, Oxfordshire. For the serpentine wall, see *Crinkle-crankle*.

Set. A slip, shoot or young plant ready for planting; hence the 'quick-set' hedge.

Shading (Victorian). A mixing of blooms in a bed so that one colour shades imperceptibly into the next.

Shadow house (sixteenth and seventeenth centuries). Former name for a small summerhouse, usually set at the end of a walk or in a corner. Larger buildings were generally described as banqueting houses.

Sham bridge (see also under *Bridge*). A structure that appears to be a bridge but is used just as a decorative termination to a piece of water as as Carshalton House, Surrey, Kenwood in London and Prior Park, Bath.

Sharawadgi. A pseudo-Chinese term suggesting elements of novelty, surprise and irregularity. Sir William Temple used it in his *Upon the Gardens of Epicurus* (1685) to denote what he claimed were such elements in Chinese gardens, although the word is derived from the Japanese not Chinese, and Chinese gardens of that time were not irregular. The term found currency in the following years, however, and Horace Walpole claimed that Richard Bateman in the 1730s was the founder of the Sharawadgi taste in England by virtue of his chinoiserie-filled garden at Old Windsor, Berkshire.

Shellwork. Shells were used to adorn French and Italian grottoes from the Renaissance onwards, and the taste spread to Britain. Some grottoes had astonishingly elaborate schemes of shell decoration: Goldney near Bristol took 25 years to complete, with a mixture of shells and corals, minerals and crystals. 200,000 English shells were used there, plus many from the East and West

Singerie: column in Italian garden, Mount Stewart, Northern Ireland.

Indies and West Africa. The task of applying shells to grotto or shell-room walls was often left to the ladies of the house: thus, at Goodwood, West Sussex, the Duke of Richmond's wife and daughter spent much time on the shell-room, while in the upper chamber of the grotto at Oatlands, Surrey, the Duchess of Newcastle was responsible for attaching the wide range of shells. Mary Delany (1700-80) achieved prodigious feats of shellwork in Ireland. Shells were sometimes applied to the columns of rotundas or other open temples, as at Stowe, Buckinghamshire.

Shred. A tree which regularly has its side branches cut off, thus promoting growth of young shoots for browsing or use as wood. See also *Coppice* and *Pollard*.

Shrubbery. A group of shrubs, i.e. low woody plants or bushes, though the term has been extended to cover flowers and trees as well. The essence of a shrubbery is that it is designed for attractiveness and display. A number of species can be mixed in the same group, and attempts are often made to mix in species which flower at different times of year. Usually they were to be found near the house, but during the eighteenth century Joseph Spence, Philip Southcote and Charles Hamilton developed the idea of taking shrubberies out into various points in the gardens so that colour would punctuate what would otherwise be a landscape of green and brown. As the number of plant introductions increased in the nineteenth century, so more varied effects could be achieved in shrubberies.

Singerie (French = monkey motifs). Although usually confined to interior decoration in the eighteenth century, e.g. Clermont's ceilings at Wentworth Castle, South Yorkshire, and in the pavilion on Monkey Island, Berkshire, the use of monkey forms, for playful or witty purposes, is found in various gardens, such as the Congreve Monument at Stowe, Buckinghamshire, or Jolivet's designs for West Wycombe, Buckinghamshire.

Skating pond. Pond designed for skating in winter, e.g. the long narrow pond at Barningham Park, County Durham.

Slip garden. A narrow garden or corridor, as at Calke Abbey, Derbyshire. The term was often applied to the ground outside the kitchen garden walls, which was cultivated for hardy vegetables and might contain manure, compost or small orchards or tree nurseries.

Souterrain. Underground passage or tunnel. Repton designed one for Ashridge, Hertfordshire, though it was executed later with the unusual feature of a series of iron arches with hooks to hang stones on. The rock underpass at Stourhead, Wiltshire, is also so named.

Species. A group of plants with similar characteristics which will normally only reproduce within that group.

Specimen tree. An unusual or interesting tree planted for effect.

Sphinx. A fairly common garden ornament, the best of which are in lead. John Cheere produced sphinxes for Chiswick, Middlesex, and Castle Hill, Devon. Sometimes the faces would be of particular persons: the (imported) sphinxes at St Paul's Walden Bury, Hertfordshire, are said to have the faces of two of Louis XV's mistresses.

Spring. (1) A source of water, often (in a garden context) feeding a lake. In some cases the spring would provide the raison d'être for a piece of garden architecture, as with Kent's cascade at the spring in Claremont, Surrey, or the elaborate spring-grotto (now much reduced) at Stourhead, Wiltshire.
(2) (medieval) A copse or plantation of young trees.

Spugne (Italian). Artificial render on walls and ceilings of Italian Renaissance garden grottoes, formed from pumice and stone to resemble stalactites.

Square. A rectangular plot or area, not necessarily square. It may be subdivided into quarters in a parterre but does not have to be. With reference to fruit and kitchen gardens, George London and Henry Wise (1710) recommended growing fruit or vegetables in squares that were from one and a half times to twice as long as they were wide, up to 160 yards (146 metres) by 80-120 (73-110 metres). Cultivation of beds within squares was said to be much easier than in an irregular shape. Town squares can often contain gardens.

Standard. (1) A tree left to grow fully in a coppice, or without other support.

(2) A large tree (sometimes as opposed to dwarf species).

Stank (Scottish). A ditch, watercourse or pool, sometimes of stagnant water.

Station. Term used by Repton and others in the Picturesque period (q.v.) to indicate a vantage point from which a 'picture' view could be enjoyed, sketched or painted.

Statuary. A sculptor or sculpture. Statuary has featured in gardens certainly since Roman times, when heroes, gods and emperors would be represented. Many Italian gardens of the Renaissance were filled with figures by the leading sculptors of the day – Donatello, Giambologna, Michelangelo. Sometimes there would be an iconographical programme, the most ambitious being at Versailles, where an elaborate allegorical scheme was directed towards the Sun King. In England statuary was prominent from the sixteenth century in formal gardens, in some cases emblematic but later more for decoration. The heyday was 1680-1780 (see *Leadwork*), when a great many finely made figures appeared, occasionally with some symbolic or associative function but mainly as garden ornaments.

Steps. At their most prominent in Italian or Italianate gardens (q.v.), steps are both utilitarian (in proceeding from one level to

Statuary: Belvoir Castle, Leicestershire.

Steps: Hestercombe House, Somerset.

another) and decorative. They may form the focal point of a garden (as in the Italian garden at Mount Edgcumbe, Cornwall) and may be dazzling in effect when produced in a series such as at Shrubland, Suffolk, or in some gardens in Italy such as the Villa Aldobrandini. Lutyens designed circular steps.

Stewpond. A fishpond, particularly associated with medieval monastic gardens, e.g. at Michelham Priory, East Sussex. In later times stewponds were sometimes used to form the basis of designed pieces of water. They produced fish for consumption whereas the later fishponds might have ornamental fish.

Stonehenge. For miniature 'Stonehenges' see *Druid temple*.

Stonework. Stone has been used extensively in Italian and other formal gardens for such things as steps, balustrading, urns, vases, fountains and statuary. In British gardens Portland stone is most commonly found, but sandstone, Bath stone and other local stone can also be seen. For composition stone, see *Coade stone* and *Pulhamite*.

Stove. A heated chamber or hothouse. In the seventeenth century they were so named because they were heated by Dutch stoves; later methods of heating included tan-bark pits and outside stoves, hot-air flues in the walls and, by 1800, hot water and steam. Humid and steamy tropical forest conditions could be produced that would foster exotic fruits and plants. They are found in most botanic gardens.

Strapwork. Ornamental work with crossed and interlaced bands.

Stumpery (Victorian). A feature composed of tree roots and stumps placed upside down into earth banks, with trailing plants festooned around them. A stumpery has been restored at Biddulph Grange,

Stumpery: Biddulph Grange, Staffordshire.

Sundial:
St Paul's
Walden Bury,
Hertfordshire.

Staffordshire, and there is another at Ickworth, Suffolk.

Sublime. The 'wild' extremity of the Picturesque. The eighteenth century, with its penchant for aesthetic and philosophical categories, saw the Sublime as awe-inspiring and provoking thoughts and feelings of dread or eternity. Wild and precipitous scenery, abysses and cataracts were the stuff of sublime landscape. In gardens there are sublime elements at Hawkstone, Shropshire (which terrified Dr Johnson); Hackfall, North Yorkshire; and Hafod, Dyfed.

Subspecies. A group of plants distinct genetically from the rest of their species.

Subtropical bedding (Victorian). The essence of subtropical bedding, a fashion imported from France and Germany, and popular 1860-90, was the display of leaves for their ornamental appearance, replacing flowers. Thus species with large, brightly coloured or variegated foliage, and often raised in greenhouses, were used:

Summerhouse: Nymans Garden, West Sussex.

canna, coleus, philodendron and even deliberately grown kale and rhubarb. The beds themselves were often irregular, as was the grouping of the foliage plants in them. John Gibson introduced plants from Paris to Battersea Park, London, to create such a garden, planting bananas and aralias.

Summerhouse. A garden pavilion intended for spending time in, particularly in fine weather. The architecture is often fanciful. They can be made to revolve, generally on a concrete base, to catch the sun as it moves round. What distinguishes a summerhouse from other garden buildings is not always clear, and the term is used somewhat arbitrarily: the summerhouse attributed to Sanderson Miller at Enville, Staffordshire (1750s), has also been called the Billiard Room or the Museum. A two-storey summerhouse (c.1780) in Gothick style at Alderley, Gloucestershire, affords fine views over the Severn valley.

Sundial. A common item in a garden for telling the time by the shadow cast by the sun. Many ornamental sundials were produced, sometimes above a sculpted figure, usually Father Time crouching down with an hourglass in one hand. Good examples of this figure are at Duncombe Park, North Yorkshire (stone), and at St Paul's Walden Bury, Hertfordshire (lead), both attributed to John Van Nost. Sundials may also be fixed to the vertical surface of a wall. A multi-faceted dial that functions also with moonlight is to be seen at Pitmedden, Grampian Region.

Sunken garden. A garden deliberately laid out at a lower level than its surroundings for ease of viewing. The sunken garden at Kensington Gardens, London (early eighteenth century), was formed out of an old gravel pit.

Swedish hut. See under *Bengal cottage*.

Swiss cottage. See next entry.

Swiss garden. A garden with real or supposed Swiss elements, including buildings and plantings. An early example was the precipitous area called Switzerland (a signpost said 'To Switzerland') at Hawkstone, Shropshire, but most examples come from the nineteenth century. There is a Swiss chalet complex at Kenwood, London, but the most famous is the Swiss Garden, Old Warden, Bedfordshire (1820s), which has a thatched chalet and tree-shelter and an extensive fir plantation. A Swiss cottage by Jeffry Wyatville (c.1815) survives at Endsleigh, Devon.

Tabernacle. A small hut or pavilion, e.g. the fishing tabernacles at Studley Royal, North Yorkshire.

Tank. Container for water. See also *Cistern*.

Tapis vert (French = green carpet). A lawn cut in a regular shape. It is often found in formal French gardens of the seventeenth century.

Taxonomy. The classification of plants (or animals), sometimes including the study of formation of species.

Tazza (Italian = cup). A shallow bowl mounted on a stem or other support with a circular base, for the display of flowers and plants. It was popular in the Victorian period: a large one supported by four lions is in Regent's Park, London.

Tea garden. In Victorian times it was fashionable for ladies to visit tea gardens in the afternoon for social purposes and to stroll in the maze which they often contained. There was a revival of the tea garden in the 1920s and 1930s, when tables were set out in orchards and gardens, with rustic furniture, for open air tea.

Tea house. A garden building in which it was intended that tea should be taken. A tea-house bridge by Robert Adam is at Audley End, Essex, and another eighteenth-century tea house graces a terrace at Iford Manor, Wiltshire. Adam also created a castellate tea pavilion at Auchincruive, Strathclyde Region.

Temperate house. A conservatory designed for the cultivation of plants that require a certain degree of heat, but not as much as tropical houses or palm houses. A well-known temperate house is at Kew, Surrey.

Tempietto (Italian = small temple). The word is usually applied to open rotundas which are modelled on Bramante's Tempietto in Montorio, Rome.

Temple. A garden building, generally in Gothic or classical style. The term can be applied to many types of garden building with

Swiss garden: tree-shelter, Old Warden, Bedfordshire.

Swiss cottage: Endsleigh, Devon.

Tabernacle: fishing tabernacle, Studley Royal, North Yorkshire.

Tea house: Iford Manor, Wiltshire.

Temple: Temple of Diana, Weston Park, Staffordshire.

Terra-cotta: Hidcote Manor Garden, Gloucestershire.

Temple: St Paul's Walden Bury, Hertfordshire.

interior space in which to stand or sit, with or without walls. Many temples have a name (Temple of Venus, Temple of Ancient Virtue) or are characterised architecturally as Gothic Temple or Doric Temple. Some may even be of rustic style, like the bark temple at Exton, Leicestershire.

Tender plant. One that needs indoor protection, particularly in winter.

Term. A classical bust capping a pedestal that tapers slightly from the top. Strictly it should represent the Roman god Terminus and be used for marking the boundary of an area or estate, but in practice the word is used interchangeably with herm (q.v.) and terms may be found anywhere in a garden, often in a group.

Terra-cotta. A kiln-baked ceramic, popular in the nineteenth century for garden ornaments such as urns and vases.

Terrace. A flat, level area, sometimes raised.

Terrace garden. A garden with one or more platforms with walks, which can be on different levels, usually close to the house. A fine example is the garden at Powis Castle, Powys, where there are three terraces at different heights, each with its own scheme of ornamentation: on one is a balustrade with lead figures of shepherds and shepherdesses. Several of the great gardens of France and Italy had terraces, since the formal style lent itself to shelf-like dispositions of walks, parterres and water. A superb series of ten terraces can be found on the island garden of Isola Bella, Lake Maggiore, Italy. A revival of the stepped terrace

Terrace garden: Powis Castle, Powys.

Terrace walk: Rievaulx Terrace, North Yorkshire.

Thatch: thatched bridge, Polesden Lacey, Surrey.

Theatre: nature theatre, Sanspareil, Bayreuth, Germany.

Topiary: Levens Hall, Cumbria.

occurred in the Victorian period, as at Westonbirt House, Gloucestershire.

Terrace walk. A feature that finds particular expression in the eighteenth-century English garden. It is a walk that may be straight or curving, level or on a slope, but the key is the view or views which the walk affords. The views might be over the grounds or, more likely, across the surrounding countryside. Oatlands, Surrey, had a straight terrace walk 1000 metres in length, looking out over the Broadwater and the Thames valley beyond. The curving walk at Rievaulx Terrace, North Yorkshire, is so contrived that it permits thirteen separate views through the trees down the cliff to the ruined abbey below, showing it from markedly different angles. The walk that curves away from the house at Castle Howard, North Yorkshire, follows the course of Henderskelfe village street, which had been removed to make way for Lord Carlisle's landscaping.

Thatch. Thatch of reed or straw has often been used to roof garden buildings, particularly those in a rustic style.

Theatre. (1) An amphitheatre (q.v.), as in Pope's reference to constructing a 'Bridgmannick theatre' in his garden. (2) A circular or semicircular land-form, possibly planted in tiers; cf. *Amphitheatre.* In his *Epistle to Lord Burlington* (1731) Pope speaks of the Genius of the Place scooping out the vale 'in circling Theatres'. (3) A set piece, such as the Water Theatre at Isola Bella, Lake Maggiore, Italy, where a great stepped and tiered structure with pilasters, water effects, shells and statuary forms an extravagant tableau with the architecture as performer. Another such is at the Villa Aldobrandini, Frascati, Italy. (4) An actual theatre, designed for open-air performance. (5) See *Auricula theatre.*

Thicket. A group of trees growing tightly together; a wilderness.

Thornery. A copse or wood of thorns (genus *Crataegus*). At Sezincote, Gloucestershire, the 'thornery' indicates where such a copse once stood. A cottage by Repton in the grounds of Woburn Abbey, Bedfordshire, was called The Thornery, because it was situated among different kinds of thorn.

T'ing. A Chinese pavilion, open in construction, with a roof but no walls or sides. Sir William Chambers designed one for Kew, Surrey (c.1760), which stood on a base in the centre of a pond. This was one of several oriental structures which formed a collection there.

Tomb garden. A Mogul garden, dominated by a tomb or mausoleum. The outstanding example is the Taj Mahal in India (completed 1654).

Tonnelle. See *Tunnel-arbour.*

Topiarius (Latin). Gardener. The word was used in a general sense, and although it has given rise to the anglicised 'topiary' the Roman gardener, usually a slave, would have attended to all aspects of gardening.

Topiary. The cutting and shaping of trees or hedges into various forms. The forms may be abstract or geometrical (globe, pyramid) or represent birds, animals or objects. The Romans clipped box into numerous shapes, and the practice was known in Britain certainly from the middle ages onwards. Popular materials have been box, juniper, privet, cypress and yew. There have been very elaborate schemes of topiary, such as at Levens Hall, Cumbria (from the 1680s), Earlshall, Fife (c.1890), Compton Wynyates, Warwickshire (1895), or the Coronation grouping (1953) at Hall Place, Bexley, Kent. Fashionable in Dutch gardens and in England in the seventeenth century, topiary became the object of derision

Tower: panorama tower, Croome Court, Worcestershire.

by Pope in 1713 and declined in importance though it continues
to intrigue many gardeners.

Tower. A tall building, often with castellation. It is usually placed
at a height in an estate to provide the most commanding view.
The labels Watch Tower and Prospect Tower indicate two main
functions, one for military purposes (rendered largely decorative
when it comes to garden architecture), the other for the view:
see also *Belvedere*. In a garden the purpose would be to present
a point of visual interest at a distance from the house and perhaps
to evoke associations of an imagined past, as at Painshill, Surrey
(Hamilton called the tower his castle), or Alfred's Tower at
Stourhead, Wiltshire, which serves a politico-ideological function
of commemorating the father of English civilisation. Towers can
be in various styles, but Gothic is favoured.

Town garden. Town gardens have, historically, tended to be regular
in layout, partly because of their smallness of scale. Both in
Bath and in London there is some evidence of what the back
gardens of town houses looked like in the eighteenth century,
with regular formations of walks, shrubs and trees.

Tree house. A construction built among the branches of a tree.
The most spectacular example in Britain is the tree house at
Pitchford Hall, Shropshire, which dates from the seventeenth
century though the rococo decoration inside is from the eighteenth.

Treillage. Trelliswork, but usually of a more elaborate kind, although
some authors use the words interchangeably. While trellis is
generally simple and small-scale, treillage can be highly
architectural, with columns, alcoves and wings, as can be found
in the grander French gardens such as Chantilly or Versailles.

Trellis. A frame for supporting climbing plants, usually of wood, constructed in cross or lattice pattern. It may arch over to form a pergola or be a straight screen or fence. See also *Arbour*.

Triumphal arch. See *Arch*.

Trompe l'oeil. An effect which deceives the eye. Illusion has often been employed in gardens for extending perspectives, making objects nearer or further away, and so on. Trompe l'oeil can take the form of a painted representation of an object, often at the end of an allée so that it is mistaken for the object itself at a distance. Batty Langley recommended the use of ruins painted on canvas to substitute for real ones, and at Vauxhall Gardens, London, there was a highly effective painting of a ruined Roman bridge at one end of the Cross Walk, and also an image of the Ruins of Palmyra at the end of the Triumphal Arch Walk. Also at Vauxhall was the cascade, an imitation where tin produced the sight and sound of water. An effect of a different sort was at Oatlands, Surrey, where the lake was so formed that it appeared to flow under the distant Walton Bridge.

Troughery. An area for a collection of stone troughs used as containers for plants, as at Rodmarton Manor, Gloucestershire.

Troy Town. A form of turf or other flat maze in which there is a

Tudor garden: modern reconstruction, Tudor House Museum, Southampton, Hampshire.

single path, rather than a choice, winding in concentric circles. Some were used for exercise, others for religious devotion. A Troy Town at Hampton Court, Middlesex, led to the later formation of the well-known hedge maze. They are common in Scandinavia.

Tudor garden. Some principal characteristics of Tudor gardens were mazes, mounts and knots. Large gardens such as that at Hampton Court, Middlesex, had elaborate sculpture in wood, of an heraldic kind, such as that re-created in the Tudor House Museum garden, Southampton, Hampshire. The term is also used for a Victorian-period revival of Tudor layout and ornamentation.

Tufa. Properly, a rock of volcanic detritus. The term has been used widely but incorrectly in gardens to describe a pitted limestone, somewhat resembling a skull, which should be called spongestone or honeycomb rock. It forms a dressing particularly to grottoes, creating a mysterious and rather eerie effect. Much of the grotto work at Fonthill, Wiltshire, for example, uses the material.

Tunnel-arbour. An extended arbour (*tonnelle* in French). A restored example is at Painswick, Gloucestershire. See also *Pergola*.

Turfed benches or seats (medieval). Raised seats or benches covered in turf, a feature of many enclosed gardens of the middle ages. The seats would be built against the wall or a central tree or fountain, and flowers would often be planted in the turf.

Turf work. When turf is cut into various shapes or designs (see *Gazon coupé*).

Turkish tent. A pavilion decorated in Turkish style. The best-known in England was designed by Henry Keene for Painshill, Surrey. A brick structure on which blue and white canvas was mounted, it was topped by a crescent moon and has been re-created there. A lesser version was at Stourhead, Wiltshire,

The Turkish Tent at Painshill.

(From left to right) *Urn: Anglesey Abbey, Cambridgeshire; Vase: Tuscan vase, Melbourne Hall, Derbyshire; Vase: Kingston Lacy, Dorset.*

but not for long. These date from the mid eighteenth century, when the craze for exotic styles was at its height (cf. Sir William Chambers's Alhambra and Mosque at Kew, Surrey). A plainer Turkish tent was at Vauxhall Gardens, London, by c.1740. They also feature memorably on the continent, e.g. at Drottningholm, Sweden, and the Désert de Retz, France.

Tuscan. See *Orders of architecture.*

Umbrello, umbrella. A light structure consisting of a central stem with a circular canopy at the top. A seat may be formed round the base of the stem. A Chinese umbrello was erected at Stourhead, Wiltshire, but did not last long. Designs for umbrellos are found in the pattern books of the eighteenth and early nineteenth centuries. More substantial umbrellas might have columns and ogee arches (Woburn Abbey, Bedfordshire) instead of the central stem.

Underplanting. The planting of low-growing shrubs and small trees within a wood. The effect is to provide colour and variety close to the ground, at a height where otherwise there would be only space or bare trunk.

Urban garden. See *Town garden.*

Urn. Urns have frequently been used to decorate a garden. They can be made of various materials, principally stone (natural or composition), lead or terra-cotta, and mounted on pedestals.

Vegetable garden: Barnsley House, Gloucestershire.

Sometimes they have a commemorative purpose, with perhaps an inscription in memory of a deceased friend, relative or famous figure. The urn and its base can be highly ornate, such as the Four Faces urn at Bramham, West Yorkshire. Many authors use 'urn' and 'vase' synonymously; an urn is often closed at the top and has a straighter, more upright shape, but this is not always the case.

Valley garden. Garden constructed along a valley, e.g. the Valley Gardens at Windsor Great Park, Berkshire. See also *Dell garden.*

Variety. Plant with different characteristics within a species or subspecies.

Vase. Like urns, vases are familiar ornaments in a garden. They can vary from plain, regular patterns to the large and exquisitely detailed early eighteenth-century Tuscan vases in lead by Van Nost to be found at Melbourne Hall, Derbyshire, and Syon House, Middlesex. Materials vary, from lead, marble, Bath stone, bronze and terra-cotta to Coade stone and iron. Decoration, and indeed style, of vases was often taken from Europe, notably Italy and France. 'Vase' and 'urn' are often used interchangeably, though in some cases vases have a bulging convex side.

Vegetable garden. An area for the cultivation of vegetables. Great attention has been paid to the arrangement of plots for particular vegetables, with many garden authors in the seventeenth and eighteenth centuries giving plans as to how a vegetable garden should be set out. A geometrical example is at Barnsley

House, Gloucestershire.

Vergier (medieval). A garden or orchard.

Vermiculation. Carved finish applied to stonework in intricate wriggling patterns like worm-tracks (vermis = worm).

Versailles case. A box-like screen or case up to a metre high with small ball or acorn finials at the corners, for containing a shrub or small tree. Sometimes the sides can be opened for root pruning and soil change.

Vertugadin (French). A grass bank in the shape of a crescent with pointed ends, somewhat in the manner of an amphitheatre, as at Chantilly.

View house. A single-storeyed building with an open window, placed on an eminence for the view.

Vinery. A garden house in which vines are cultivated. A particularly

Versailles case: Blenheim Palace, Oxfordshire.

Vermiculation: Bowood, Wiltshire.

Vinery: Holkham Hall, Norfolk.

Viridiarium: House of the Vettii, Pompeii, Italy.

attractive example is Samuel Wyatt's at Holkham Hall, Norfolk
(1780), with its central entrance of two white Ionic columns and
a wrought-iron fanlight above. Other fruit trees were also grown
in it, and it was used for evening parties in the summer, being
described by one visitor as a 'graceful little paradise'.

Vineyard. An area, generally on a slope, for growing vines. Within
a garden it can be made to be a decorative feature as well, as at
Painshill, Surrey, where Charles Hamilton planned his vineyard
above a water meadow, later to become an arm of the lake.

Virectum (medieval). A green area used as a pleasure ground. In
classical Latin the word is *viretum*, a lawn or turf.

Virgultum (medieval). A plantation of young trees or coppice.
See also *Spring*.

Viridarium (Roman and medieval). An open green space, with
some plantings, used for pleasure and recreation. In the middle
ages it generally represented a large garden area (in contrast to
the small enclosed hortus conclusus or herbarium) where trees
would be grown for appearance and for fruit.

Viridiarium (Roman). A small garden, within the peristyle of a
Roman villa. It was intended for the display of individual plants,
many of which would be shaped to become living furniture or
architecture.

Vista. In its simplest meaning, a view. In garden design it is a deliberately created and controlled view, perhaps framed by trees, at the end of an allée, or determined by land-form, for example between two islands in a lake. The essence of a vista is distance: the spectator's view is focused on an object or scene, sometimes with tricks of perspective to make it look nearer or further. Vistas may occur equally in the grand formal kind of garden such as Versailles or in a naturalistic landscape garden such as Painshill, Surrey, where objects appear and reappear unexpectedly in a circuit of 'hide and reveal'. See also *Prospect*.

Volary, volery (or French, volière). An aviary or bird-garden, as formerly at Chiswick and Hampton Court (both Middlesex).

Walk. A path (traditionally of grass, gravel or sand) within a garden and intended for walking on, either for gentle exercise, for social purposes or to view the garden. A walk should be even and level. Sand walks were common, particularly in the eighteenth century. The advantage of gravel was that it dried out quickly. Other materials such as tarmac have been used in more recent times.

Wall. In gardens, walls are generally for horticultural purposes, to protect plants within their enclosure and to have fruit grown against them. They can be decorative (see *Walled garden* and *Crinkle-crankle*), made of various materials, and can be heated by internal flues.

Walled garden. In Britain the walled garden has tended to be a

Walled garden: double walled garden, Luffness, Lothian.

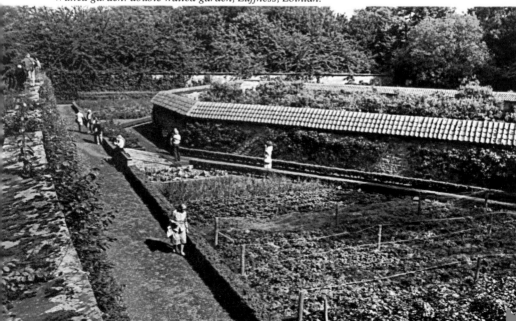

Water garden: Studley Royal, North Yorkshire.

relatively small area for a specific purpose, from medieval monasteries with herb gardens for food and medicine to the later development of flower and kitchen gardens. Some walls, traditionally of brick, are very fine structures in themselves, such as Vanbrugh's kitchen garden at Blenheim, Oxfordshire, punctuated by handsome door arches and surmounted by finials, and at Castle Howard, North Yorkshire.

Wardian case. Nathaniel Ward (1791-1868) pioneered the use of sealed glass cases for transporting plants from abroad. They were later also used for purposes of indoor display. Until the 1830s the mortality rate for plants sent on long journeys had been high: then, through use of the Wardian case, their chances of survival were increased dramatically. The principle was that the plants within the case produced moisture that would condense on the inside walls and be recycled. As a result the number of exotics introduced into Britain proliferated.

Watchtower. See *Tower.*

Waterfall. Similar to cascade (q.v.) but more usually used for natural falls, quite often on a large scale. Natural falls are displayed to advantage at Hafod, Dyfed, while William Emes constructed an unusual cylindrical waterfall in 1774 at Erddig, Clwyd, now known as the 'Cup-and-Saucer.'

Water garden. Since the gardens of antiquity in the Middle East, water has played a central role in gardens, for both irrigation and ornamentation. A water garden, however, is either an area within a garden in which water provides the main interest, with rocks, pools, cascades and a display of moisture-loving plants, or a large garden where water is the dominant feature, such as Studley Royal, North Yorkshire, with its river and Moon Ponds, or Hodnet Hall, Shropshire, with its interconnecting pools and lake (although a single pool there is called the water garden for its particular construction and planting).

Water theatre. See *Theatre*.

Water tower. A tower containing a tank or reservoir so that water can be supplied to a house, etc. by gravity. An impressive early eighteenth-century example is at Carshalton House, Surrey, attributed to Henry Joynes; another is at Goldney, Bristol.

Waterwheel. Waterwheels have been used to raise water in a garden for the purpose of feeding fountains or maintaining lakes. Fourteen gigantic wheels forced water from the river Seine up to the Aqueduc de Marly, which supplied 1400 fountains at Versailles. The waterwheel at Painshill, Surrey, was an ingenious contrivance said to have been devised by the owner, Charles Hamilton, though possibly based on classical models. Water was scooped up from the river Mole through leather pipes to a hollow axle in the centre, which fed a trough leading eventually to the lake, several metres higher than the river. The present device at Painshill dates from the 1830s, a magnificent cast-iron wheel 12 metres in diameter which activates pumps that lift water from

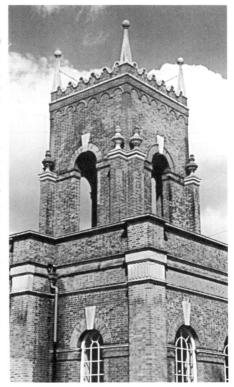

Water tower: Carshalton House, Surrey.

Waterworks: Lower Grotto, Ermitage, Bayreuth, Germany.

the river.

Waterworks. The controlling of water, often referred to as hydraulics, fascinated many of the designers and engineers of Italian Renaissance and classical French gardens. Fountains are the obvious expression of this love: the Villa d'Este has an assortment, including the pathway of the Hundred Fountains. Other uses were to provide artificial cascades, water effects in grottoes and giochi d'acqua (q.v.).

Well-head. Well-heads might be ornate enough to be decorative garden structures in their own right. Sometimes, indeed, they were solely decorative and did not stand above a well. The best designs came from Italy, where the well-head would have an external facing that was moulded or carved. In Britain many well-heads were imported from Italy, while others were Italian in style. Examples can be seen at Cirencester House, Gloucestershire, and Hestercombe, Somerset. The commonest material was marble.

Well house. A building to cover and shelter a well, as at Hales Place, Kent.

Wilderness. Basically a designed grove or wood with paths cut through it (cf. *Bosquet*). The essence of a wilderness is that it is ornamental, an attractive area in which to wander or pause. In formal gardens it was laid out at some distance from the house,

Well-head: Gilbert White's garden, Selborne, Hampshire.

Well house: Hales Place, Kent.

beyond the parterre. The shape of the grove was usually regular though the design within it could be varied. Trees were generally laid out in rows (e.g Wilton House, Wiltshire, 1630s, or Kirby Hall, Northamptonshire, late seventeenth century). At Ham House, Surrey (1671), the now restored wilderness comprises an area with several paths and compartments delineated by hornbeam

Wilderness: Ham House, Surrey.

hedges. These compartments contain some trees behind the hedges but are also quite open, with grass, flowering shrubs, paths, seats and statuary. Trees and shrubs in a wilderness could be of many different species mixed together. By the early eighteenth century paths wriggled and wound, and at Wray Wood, Castle Howard, North Yorkshire, straight allées were converted into serpentine paths. Later on, in the more naturalistic landscapes of the late eighteenth and early nineteenth centuries, a wilderness would be an informal woodland area of mixed species.

Wild garden. (1) A garden where wild (woodland and meadow) flowers and plants grow in an apparently natural way.

(2) The term is more specifically applied to the type of garden described by William Robinson in *The Wild Garden* (1870) and also by Gertrude Jekyll in some of her writings. Wildness did not mean disorder, nor the use of wild species only, but a mixture of wild and cultivated hardy plants (including exotic and subtropical, q.v.) according to the situation – woodland, heath, waterside – but usually in the rougher parts of the grounds, where they will 'flourish without the slightest attention after once being planted' (Robinson). So far from being wild, the Robinsonian or Jekyllian garden exhibits tightness of control and a unifying design scheme. Individual species were grouped and massed, and wild plants were brought in to spread, sometimes with unfortunate results, since a few are now regarded as weeds.

Window box. To those who imagine that the window box is a modern development to suit the needs of urban life, it may come as a surprise to know that they were widely used in medieval times. A range of plants can be grown in window boxes: herbs, bulbs, bedding plants and even dwarf conifers.

Winter garden. (1) An area planted for winter display, with evergreens or winter-flowering plants.

(2) A large glasshouse for public entertainment. A number have survived at seaside resorts such as Blackpool, Lancashire; Eastbourne, East Sussex; and Great Yarmouth, Norfolk. The original purpose of displaying plants during the winter has disappeared or been minimalised.

Woodland garden. A garden created within woodland, therefore usually on acid soil, with imported species such as camellias, magnolias, hydrangeas and rhododendrons that grow in woodland in their native country. Good examples are Bodnant, Gwynedd, and Leonardslee, West Sussex.

Woodwork. An area containing a plantation of trees, e.g. within the early eighteenth-century military garden at Blenheim,

Oxfordshire, where a formal wilderness contained clipped shrubs and evergreens.

Wrought iron. See *Ironwork.*

Yaird (Scottish). Garden, especially a cottage or kitchen garden attached to the house.

Zigzag. A path with alternate left and right turnings at sharp angles, usually to aid the ascent and descent of a steep slope. At Mount Edgcumbe, Cornwall, there is a spectacular example, originally visible from a distance and intended to be a prominent feature, which is said to have terrified the ladies in the eighteenth century. There is also a notable one at Stourhead, Wiltshire, where the Hermitage provided an 'incident' along the way.

Zoological garden (usually shortened to zoo). A garden or other open-air area for the keeping, display and study of animals, most of which are native to other countries. The concept of the zoo goes back to antiquity (see also *Menagerie*), but the name and the present public perception date from the nineteenth century. Many large cities have one, despite problems of space, and they are a great visitor attraction.

The Zigzag at Brantwood, John Ruskin's home in Cumbria.

Appendix

SOME MAJOR BRITISH GARDEN DESIGNERS

In the text of the glossary a number of designers are mentioned who feature prominently in garden history. Below are listed some major names with brief details of dates, significance and principal works.

BARRY, Sir Charles (1795-1860). He is remembered for establishing the Italianate garden in Victorian England, notably at Trentham Park, Staffordshire; Cliveden, Buckinghamshire; Shrubland, Suffolk. He employed Italian Renaissance garden features of terracing, balustrades, staircases, urns and fountains. Another terrace can be seen at Harewood House, West Yorkshire.

BRIDGEMAN, Charles (?-1738). A designer who stands at the crossover from geometrical late baroque to the landscape garden: he was still a formalist in overall plan but introduced outside country scenery (cf. *Forest gardening*) and was the first to exploit the possibilities of the ha-ha. His range of commissions was extensive, including the royal parks; Claremont, Surrey; Stowe, Buckinghamshire; Wimpole, Cambridgeshire; Rousham, Oxfordshire. In many cases, however, his work was remodelled by later designers such as Kent or Brown. He was Royal Gardener 1728-38.

BROWN, Lancelot (1716-83). Known widely as 'Capability' Brown, he was the first landscape design consultant in the fully professional sense of the term, undertaking about two hundred commissions. He worked to something of a formula (see *Brownian*) but was responsible not only for putting his ideas about the naturalistic landscape park into practice on an extensive scale but for inculcating and spreading the taste for such scenery. Especially attractive among his many works are: Blenheim, Oxfordshire; Chatsworth, Derbyshire; Petworth, West Sussex; Weston Park, Staffordshire; Longleat, Wiltshire.

EVELYN, John (1620-1705). A writer on all aspects of practical gardening: his most famous work was *Sylva* (1664), a treatise on forestry. He designed gardens at Sayes Court, Kent (his own); Wotton, Surrey (for his brother); Albury Park, Surrey; Euston Hall, Suffolk; and others.

GILPIN, William Sawrey (1762-1843). A landscape designer who followed the Picturesque tenets of Uvedale Price. He used a wider range of trees than his predecessors and was equally at home with regular or irregular layouts. The lakeside garden at Clumber, Nottinghamshire, is his.

HAMILTON, The Hon. Charles (1704-86). Famed as the owner and designer of Painshill, Surrey, from 1738 to 1773, he developed Kent's ideas about pictorial gardening to a high degree of charm and sophistication. His circuit provided changes of view and mood, set pieces, illusion and surprise. He was keenly interested in plantings, particularly newly obtained species from North America. He advised also at Holland Park, London; Bowood and Fonthill, Wiltshire. He retired to Bath, where his town garden was regarded as exemplary.

JEKYLL, Gertrude (1843-1932). An author and designer of gardens with a particular love of planting in the cottage-garden tradition. She is well-known for her partnership with the architect Edwin Lutyens, which lasted from 1889 until her death. As an artist before she took up planting design, she was deeply interested in colour and the relationship of blooms of one colour with those of another. Her work included her own garden at Munstead Wood, Surrey; Orchards, Surrey; Hestercombe, Somerset.

JELLICOE, Sir Geoffrey (1900-). An outstanding twentieth-century landscape architect who has deep concern and regard for historical styles and movements although he has also been involved in modernism. Some of the historical influence can be seen in his reshaping of the formal garden at Ditchley, Oxfordshire; St Paul's Walden Bury, Hertfordshire; Sutton Place, Surrey. A large park containing areas representing different countries and styles has been created in Texas.

KENT, William (1685-1748). After a formative decade in Italy, Kent, who tried his hand at all the visual arts, returned to England full of Italian ideas of scenery and architecture. They were, however, tempered by his experiments with the Gothic style. He approached garden design as an artist, sketching scenes and creating a series of painterly compositions in three dimensions, with emphasis on light and shade, groves and lawn, slopes and naturalistic water. His many commissions included Chiswick, Middlesex; Claremont, Surrey; Esher Place, Surrey; Euston Hall, Suffolk; Holkham, Norfolk;

Kensington Gardens, London; Richmond Gardens, Surrey; Rousham, Oxfordshire; Shotover, Oxfordshire; Stowe, Buckinghamshire.

LANGLEY, Batty (1696-1751). Remembered more for his architectural and gardening treatises than for his commissions, though he designed the Bowling Green Temple at Wrest Park, Bedfordshire. While still largely a formalist, he shares with Bridgeman and Switzer a vision of the countryside outside the garden and a wish to bring it into the view. See *Artinatural*.

LONDON, George (?-1714). One of the last of the formal, baroque-style designers. He was much influenced by visits to France. He designed several gardens in partnership with William Talman, the architect, notably Wanstead, Essex; Chatsworth, Derbyshire; Dyrham, Avon. He laid out Kensington Gardens, London, in 1691. He established a pre-eminent nursery at Brompton Park, London, in partnership with Henry Wise.

LOUDON, John Claudius (1783-1843). A prolific author and designer, his writings are his chief memorial, ranging from encyclopedias to the first magazines exclusively concerned with gardening. He followed some picturesque principles derived from Uvedale Price, but his early passion for irregularity was modified by acknowledgement that there was a place for regular gardens, particularly if based on history. He also advocated the gardenesque approach to planting.

LUTYENS, Sir Edwin (1869-1944). Architect and garden designer. Many of his garden works were achieved in collaboration with Gertrude Jekyll: he chose the main lines and designed the architectural features, while she planned the plantings. He believed that every garden scheme should have a central idea, to which all features should relate. The house was often responsible for determining this central idea. Apart from the Jekyll gardens, Lutyens's finest garden achievement was at Tyringham, Buckinghamshire.

MASON, William (1725-81). Poet and garden designer. His poem in four books, *The English Garden* (1772-81), sought to base garden design on a poet's feeling and a painter's eye. He did small-scale work for his friends and is best remembered for the flower garden at Nuneham Courtenay, Oxfordshire, in which irregular informality of flower beds was combined with morality and poetic sentiment.

MAWSON, Thomas (1861-1933). His style evolved from the Arts and Crafts movement to a characteristic use of formal terraces leading gradually to more natural areas and views, as at Graythwaite Hall, Cumbria. He also designed public parks and worked extensively abroad.

NESFIELD, William Andrews (1793-1881). A designer who utilised designs from sixteenth- and seventeenth-century gardening books to create suitable parterre gardens for houses of those periods. His work has often suffered subsequent alteration, but his main commissions were at Holkham, Norfolk; Blickling Hall, Norfolk; Kew, Surrey (the area surrounding the Palm House); Broughton Hall, North Yorkshire. He laid out a geometrical pattern of shaped trees at Witley Court, Worcestershire.

PAGE, Russell (1906-85). A leading English landscape architect, although most of the work of his maturity was carried out abroad. He planned the Festival Gardens in Battersea Park, London, in 1951.

PAXTON, Sir Joseph (1803-65). The designer of the great Victorian works at Chatsworth, Derbyshire (including the rock garden and fountains) and several of the new public parks at Liverpool, Birkenhead, Halifax, Southport and the Crystal Palace.

PETO, Harold (1854-1933). An architect and collector who was deeply influenced by formal Italian gardens. He brought back from Italy many decorative objects – cisterns, sarcophagi, statuary – and then set them in formal gardens with buildings, urns and staircases to match. This is exemplified best in his own garden of Iford Manor, Wiltshire, but Buscot Park, Oxfordshire, has an impressive water garden combined with allées and much sculpture. West Dean, West Sussex, is an attractive example of his work.

REPTON, Humphry (1752-1818). The successor to Brown from 1788, Repton followed many of Brown's ideas for large-scale parkscape but differed in bringing flower gardens, often quite formal in character, back near the house. He shared some of the ideas of the Picturesque school, but rejected their insistence on the parallels between painting and scenery. He set out his principles in written form. See *Red Book, Approach, Drive.* Among a large number of works may be cited Attingham Park, Shropshire; Ashridge, Hertfordshire; Kenwood, London; Cobham Hall, Kent; Sheringham, Norfolk.

ROBINSON, William (1838-1935). An Irish writer and gardener who moved to London in 1861. He is particularly associated with the idea of the wild garden and with informal mixtures of cultivated and wild species, native and exotic. His own garden at Gravetye Manor, West Sussex, has an area of woodland around alpine and flower gardens with many specimen trees. His planting plans there were revived from 1958.

SWITZER, Stephen (1682-1745). After apprenticeship with George London, Switzer went to Blenheim, Oxfordshire, to work with Vanbrugh and Wise. Among his own layouts are Grimsthorpe, Lincolnshire, and Nostell Priory, West Yorkshire. He wrote the influential *Ichnographia Rustica* (1718), which set out his central precept of grand axial lines that would join the house and the estate. The perfect example of the theory implemented is Cirencester Park, Gloucestershire. See *Forest gardening*.

VANBRUGH, Sir John (1664-1726). A man of great versatility, but famed for his plays and his architecture. His place as a designer of garden layouts is difficult to determine, because he frequently worked with Bridgeman and others, but his vision and foresight in anticipating romanticism and the Picturesque are remarkable. He is remembered for his astonishing mock fortifications and other buildings at Castle Howard, North Yorkshire; for the palace and bridge at Blenheim, Oxfordshire; the Belvedere at Claremont, Surrey; and the Rotunda at Duncombe Park, North Yorkshire.

WISE, Henry (1653-1738). Like his partner George London, he was one of the last of the baroque school. He was master gardener to Queen Anne and worked extensively on the royal parks, particularly Hampton Court and Kensington Gardens. At Blenheim, Oxfordshire, he designed the huge military garden.

WRIGHT, Thomas (1711-86). An individualistic (not to say eccentric) designer of garden buildings in various styles, especially rustic, and elaborate flower gardens in the rococo style. His work is well displayed at Badminton, Avon; Shugborough, Staffordshire; Stoke Gifford, Avon; Hampton Court House, Middlesex.

Further reading

GENERAL
Adams, W. H. *Nature Perfected*. Abbeville Press, 1991.
Brown, Jane. *The Art and Architecture of English Gardens*. Weidenfeld & Nicolson, 1989.
Hobhouse, Penelope. *Plants in Garden History*. Pavilion, 1994.
Hunt, John Dixon, and Willis, Peter. *The Genius of the Place: The English Landscape Garden 1620-1820*. MIT, revised edition 1988.
Mosser, M., and Teyssot, G. (editors). *The History of Garden Design*. Thames & Hudson, 1991.
The Oxford Companion to Gardens. Oxford University Press, 1986.
Thacker, Christopher. *The History of Gardens*. Croom Helm, 1979 (subsequently paperback).

PERIODS OF BRITISH GARDENS
Brown, Jane. *The English Garden in Our Time*. Antique Collectors Club, 1986.
Elliott, Brent. *Victorian Gardens*. Batsford, 1986 (subsequently paperback).
Harvey, John. *Medieval Gardens*. Batsford, 1981 (subsequently paperback).
Jacques, David. *Georgian Gardens: The Reign of Nature*. Batsford, 1983 (subsequently paperback).
Ottewill, David. *The Edwardian Garden*. Yale University Press, 1989.
Strong, Roy. *The Renaissance Garden in England*. Thames & Hudson, 1979 (subsequently paperback).

PARTICULAR COUNTRIES AND STYLES
Adams, W. H. *The French Garden 1500-1800*. Scolar, 1979.
Hunt, John Dixon. *Garden and Grove: The Italian Renaissance Garden in the English Imagination, 1600-1750*. Princeton University Press, 1986.
Laird, Mark. *The Formal Garden*. Thames & Hudson, 1992.
Lazzaro, Claudia. *The Italian Renaissance Garden*. Yale University Press, 1990.
Woodbridge, Kenneth. *Princely Gardens: The Origins and Development of the French Formal Style*. Thames & Hudson, 1986.

For current scholarship, see *Garden History* (the journal of the Garden History Society) and *Studies in the History of Gardens and Designed Landscapes* (Taylor & Francis).

Index of people and places

Page numbers in italic refer to illustrations

Abbotswood 43
Abney Park 31
Adam, Robert 19, 47, 48, 59, 75, 83, 103, 115
Addison, Joseph 80
Albury Park 136
Alderley 114
Alnwick Castle 19
Alps 9
Alton Towers *60,* 78, 85
America 9, 93, 107, 137
American Museum 12
Amesbury 25
Anglesey Abbey *74,* 90, *125*
Antony *13*
Archer, Thomas 89
Argyll, Duke of 98
Arkadia *11,* 11, 12
Arley Hall 48
Ascott 52
Ashburnham 28
Ashridge 10, 102, 110, 139
Athelhampton 44
Attingham Park 18, 139
Auchincruive 115
Audley End 47, 103, 115
Austen, Jane 98
Babylon 63
Bacon, Francis 79
Badminton 14, 66, 102, 140
Bakewell, Robert 69
Barningham Park 110
Barnsley House *126,* 126
Barry, Sir Charles 136
Bartram, John and William 9, 93
Bateman, Richard 33, 108
Bath 108, 122, 137
Battersea Park 95, 114, 139
Beckford, William 10
Beddington 81
Bedgebury Pinetum 92
Belcombe Court 100
Belfast Botanic Gardens *86*
Belsay 95, 96
Belton House *46*
Belvoir Castle *111*
Berkeley Castle *23,* 23
Bicton Park 37, 73, 83, 85, 105
Biddick Hall *10,* 11
Biddulph Grange 45, *45,* 55, *57, 112,* 112
Birkenhead 95, 139
Bishop Auckland *42,* 42
Blackpool 134
Blaise Castle 11, 44
Blaise Hamlet 39, *41,* 41, 74
Blenheim Palace 16, 25, 28, *35,* 41, 72, 76,

102, *127,* 130, 134, 136, 140
Blickling Hall 83, 96, 139
Boboli 10, *60,* 61
Bodnant 26, 134
Bomarzo 22, 69
Bonomi, Joseph 96
Boughton Monchelsea Place *42*
Bowood 12, 69, 75, 83, *100,* 100, *127,* 137
Bramante, Donato 103, 115
Bramham Park 27, 81, 88, 103, 126
Bransbury 98
Brantwood *135*
Bridgeman, Charles 10, 63, 136, 138, 140
Brighton 38, 68, 89, 98
Bristol 76
Brompton Park 138
Brondesbury 98
Broughton Hall 139
Brown, Lancelot ('Capability') 5, 18, 25, 28, 34, 40, 41, 67, 72, 85, 91, 136, 139
Burghley House *24*
Burgundy 46
Burke, Edmund 18
Burlington, 3rd Earl of 19, 42, 88, 121
Burton, Decimus 85
Burton Agnes Hall *56*
Buscot Park 139
Bushy Park 14, 93, 103
Calke Abbey *13,* 13, *38,* 54, *92,* 110
Cambridge 36
Campbell, Colen 42
Canada 102
Capel Manor 70
Carew, Sir Francis 81
Carlisle, 3rd Earl of 120
Carpenter, Andrew 73
Carshalton House 108, 131, *131*
Castle Hill 73, 110
Castle Howard 23, 30, 34, 61, 75, *75,* 81, 90, 96, *97,* 103, 108, 120, 130, 134, 140
Chambers, Sir William 9, 11, 29, 33, 78, 83, 84, 85, 90, 104, 121, 125
Chantilly 122, 127
Charlecote Park 55
Chatsworth 23, 28, *29, 36,* 37, 55, 58, 65, 74, 136, 138, 139
Cheere, John 73, 110
Chelsea Physic Garden 90-1

Chepstow Castle 30, 58
Chirk Castle *54*
Chiswick House 15, 21, 23, 29, *42,* 45, 47, *65,* 65, 81, *88,* 88, *91,* 110, 129, 137
Cirencester Park 14, 51, 72, 99, 101, 132, 140
Clandon Park *61*
Claremont 10, 19, *20,* 23, 62, 81, 99, *110,* 110, 136, 137, 140
Clark, Frank 5
Claude Lorraine 18, 26, 34, 104
Claverton Manor 12, *13*
Clermont, Andien de 109
Cliveden 10, 27, *106,* 136
Clumber Park 18, 23, 55, *56,* 74, 137
Coade, Eleanor 34
Cobham Hall 41, 54, 139
Collinson, Peter 9
Compton Wynyates 121
Corsham Court 16, *16*
Cotehele 40, 44
Courteenhall 38
Creech Grange 47
Croome Court *122*
Croxdale Hall 93
Crystal Palace 139
Culpeper, Nicholas 65
Culzean Castle *19,* 26
D'Argenville, Dezallier 10, 63
Dashwood, Sir Francis 75
Dawley 47
Deanery Garden 43
Deans Court *41*
Delany, Mary 109
Désert de Retz 70, 105, 125
Dirnanean 14
Ditchley 137
Dodington House 66
Donatello 111
Donowell, John 75
Downton 91
Dropmore 14
Drottningholm 125
Drumlanrig 78, 105
Drummond Castle 85
Dughet, Gaspard 27
Duncombe Park *101,* 102, 114, 140
Dunmore 50
Dyrham 138
Earlshall 121
Eastbourne 134
Eaton Hall 88
Edinburgh: Royal Botanic Garden 99
Edzell Castle *87*
Egypt 76
Emes, William 130

Endsleigh 39, *39,* 115, *116*
Enville 21, 79, 114
Erddig 27, *27, 48,* 130
Ermenonville 105
Ermitage *132*
Esher Place 137
Euston Hall 34, 107, *107,* 136, 137
Evelyn, John 136
Exton 118
Farnborough Hall 16, 54, 89
Felbrigg Hall *43*
Fleming, John 27
Fontainebleau 86
Fonthill 10, 21, 40, 91, 124, 137
Fountains Abbey 99, 103
Foxley 92
Frascati 55
Frink, Elisabeth 107
Garrick, David *1,* 2, 66
Generalife 78, *87,* 88
Gerard, John 65
Germany 58, 102, 113
Giambologna 111
Gibbs, James 59
Gibside 15, 37
Gibson, John 114
Gilpin, William 51, 91, 137
Glynllifon 40
Goldney 16, *17, 38,* 62, 108, 131
Goodwood 109
Gravetye Manor 140
Graythwaite Hall 139
Great Saxham Hall 34
Great Yarmouth 134
Green Park 103
Greenwich 69, 103
Greville, Charles 36
Grey's Court 76
Grimsthorpe 16, 140
Guildford 102
Gunnersbury Park 107
Hackfall 15, 29, 113
Haddo House 90
Hadspen *105*
Hafod 113, 130
Hagley Hall 25, 30, *31*
Hales Place 132, *133*
Halifax 139
Hall Barn 93, 102
Hall Place 121
Halswell 102
Ham House 34, *80,* 93, 133, *133*
Hamilton, Charles 5, 66, 104, 109, 122, 128, 131, 137
Hampton *1,* 2
Hampton Court 14, 18, 27, *33,* 34, 69, 71, 76, 79, 95, 96, 103, 106, 124, 129, 140

Hampton Court House 100, 140
Harewood House 136
Hartwell House 12, 47
Hatfield House 72
Hathaway's, Anne, Cottage *40*
Hawksmoor, Nicholas 75, 90
Hawkstone 20, 113, 115
Hepworth, Barbara 107
Hestercombe House *43*, 43, *111*, 132, 137
Het Loo 44, *93*, 93
Heveningham Hall 40
Hever Castle 62, *68*, 77
Hibberd, Shirley 96, 106
Hidcote Manor Garden *117*
Hill Pasture 77
Himalayas 93
Hoare, Henry 41
Hodnet Hall 131
Hogarth, William 18, 107
Holford, R.S. 5, 83
Holker Hall 50
Holkham Hall 34, 54, 66, 81, *127*, 128, 137, 139
Holland, Henry 41
Holland Park 137
Hooker, Sir Joseph 93
Horton 76
Horton Court *8*, 9
House of Dun *53*
Hussey, Christopher 5
Hyde Park 103
Ickworth 113
Iford Manor 30, *31*, *61*, 106, 115, *117*, 139
Ilton 44, *45*
India 121
Inkpen Old Rectory 88
Ireland 43, 109
Isola Bella 81, 118, 121
Jekyll, Gertrude 134, 137, 138
Jellicoe, Sir Geoffrey 101, 137
Johnson, Samuel 113
Jolivet, M.L. 110
Joynes, Henry 131
Kedleston Hall 48, 76
Keene, Henry 124
Kemp, Edward 54
Kensington 102
Kensington Gardens 79, 103, 108, 114, 138, 140
Kent, William 12, 18, 34, 47, 59, 81, 89, 95, 103, 107, 108, 110, 136, 137
Kentwell Hall *64*
Kenwood 23, 83, 108, 115, 139
Kew 9, 22, 33, 65, 68, 71, 78, 83, 84, 85, *86*, 90, 93, 102, 104, 115, 121, 125, 139
Killerton 105

Kingston Lacy *125*
Kinmel Park 52
Kirby Hall 133
Knight, Richard Payne 18, 91
Lambeth 34, 72
Lamport Hall 58
Landsberg, Sylvia 71
Lane, Joseph and Josiah 62
Langley, Batty 12, 81, 108, 123, 138
Lansdowne, 1st Marquess of 75
Larmer Tree Gardens 20
Leasowes 47, *103*, 104
Le Corbusier 101
Leeds Castle 58
Leeswood 34
Le Notre, André 86
Leonardslee 134
Levens Hall *120*, 121
Leverhulme, 1st Viscount 71
Linderhof 71, *71*
Linnaeus, Carolus 20
Liverpool 95, 139
Loddiges, George 31
Logan Botanic Garden 22
Londesborough 42
London 9, 75, 94, 103, 122, 140 (see also specific places, parks and gardens)
London, George 98, 110, 138, 140
Longleat 55, 136
Loudon, John Claudius 31, 54, 67, 95, 138
Luffness *129*
Luton Hoo 61, 83
Lutyens, Sir Edwin 13, 43, 112, 137, 138
Manchester 95
Manderston *8*
Margam Park *81*
Marie-Antoinette 63
Marino 29, *30*
Marly, Aqueduc de 131
Marx, Roberto Burle 101
Mary, Virgin 66, 75
Marybone 84
Marylebone 94
Mason, William 50, 138
Mawson, Thomas 71, 139
Melbourne Hall 21, *68*, 69, 73, *125*, 126
Mertoun Gardens *45*
Michelangelo 111
Michelham Priory 112
Miller, Philip 7, 62, 65, 72, 73, 85, 93, 96
Miller, Sanderson 30, 47, 53, 59, 79, 104, 114
Milton Lodge *3*
Milton Park 70
Mollet, André 86, 93
Monkey Island 110
Montacute House 39, 55, *57*

Montorio 103, 115
Moore, Henry 107
Morocco 93
Morris, William 12
Mount Edgcumbe 10, 18, *82*, 83, 91, 104, 112, 135
Mount Stewart *109*
Mowbray Point 15
Munstead Wood 137
Museum of Garden History 72
Muskau 39
Nash, John 41
Nesfield, William A. 80, 88, 139
Netherlands 93
Newby Hall *21*, 22
Newcastle, Duchess of 109
New College, Oxford 36, 79
New Forest 51
Newhailes 53
Newstead Abbey *70*, *97*
North Africa 69, 98
North America 9, 93, 137
Nostell Priory 34, *35*, 77, 140
Nuneham Courtenay 50, 138
Nymans Garden *114*
Oatlands 36, 62, 72, 109, 120, 123
Old Warden 115, *116*
Old Windsor 108
Orchards 137
Osterley Park *82*
Oxburgh Hall *78*
Oxford: Botanic Garden 22; college gardens 36, 79
Packwood House 16, 18, *19*, *36*
Page, Russell 139
Paine, James 23
Painshill 5, 10, 12, 16, 23, *32*, 62, 66, 72, 104, *104*, 122, 124, *124*, 128, 129, 131, 137
Painswick Rococo Garden 40, *41*, *46*, 47, 100, 107, 124
Palestrina 95
Palladio, Andrea 23, 88
Paris 114; Jardin des Plantes 58, 72
Park Place 10
Paxton, Sir Joseph 37, 95, 139
Pennsylvania 9, 93
Penrhyn Castle 66
Peto, Harold 30, 90, 139
Petworth 18, 34, 136
Piercefield 30, 44
Pitchford Hall 122
Pitmedden 114
Pliny the Elder 9
Polesden Lacey *119*
Pompeii *128*
Pope, Alexander 5, 55,

61, 80, 81, 90, 122
Port Eliot 11
Poussin, Nicolas 27, 104
Powis Castle *67*, 73, 118, *119*
Price, Sir Uvedale 18, 91, 137, 138
Prince Regent 84, 95
Prior Park 25, 108
Priory Garden, Dunster 44
Pulham, James 95
Raby Castle *17*, 47, *48*
Ranelagh Gardens 94
Rea, John 45, 53
Regent's Park 95, 103, 115
Repton, Humphry 5, 10, 11, 44, 48, 67, 74, 90, 92, 98, 102, 110, 111, 121, 139
Richmond: Gardens 138: Palace 69; Park 103
Richmond, Duchess of 109
Rievaulx Abbey 103
Rievaulx Terrace 84, 103, *119*, 120
Rimini 23
Riskins Park 47
Robins, Thomas 38
Robinson, William 134, 140
Rodmarton Manor 123
Rome 76, 80, 81, 103, 115
Rousham 10, 12, 16, 44, 47, 63, 95, *97*, 99, 107, 108, 136, 138
Royal Pavilion, Brighton 38, 68, 98, 98
Ruskin, John 12
Russia 28, 58, 92
Sackville College, East Grinstead 33
St Germain-en-Laye 14, 23
St James's Park 21, 103
St Paul's Walden Bury 88, 110, *113*, 114, *118*, 137
Salford 95
Salisbury, Marchioness of 72
Saltram 83
Salusbury, Lady 98
Sandringham *86*
Sanspareil *119*
Sanssouci 33
Sapperton 51
Savill Gardens 21
Sayes Court 136
Scandinavia 107, 123
Schönbusch *28*
Schwetzingen 78
Scotland 44, 85, 105
Selborne *62*, 63, *133*
Serpentine, The 108
Seville cathedral *79*
Sezincote *67*, 68, 121
Shenstone, William 104
Sheringham 139

Shobden Arches *50*
Shotover *81*, 81, 138
Shrubland 69, 112, 136
Shugborough *4*, 12, 33, *35*, 104, 140
Sissinghurst Castle 40, 102
Sloane, Sir Hans 65
Somerleyton Hall 37
Somerset House 69
Somerton 72
Southampton 71, *123*, 124
Southcote, Philip 104, 109
Southport 139
Sovereign House, Pimlico 68
Spain 69, 77
Spence, Joseph 109
Spetchley Park 102
Stainborough Castle 30
Stoke Gifford 140
Stonehenge 44
Stourhead 5, 18, *19*, 19, 23, 41, 44, 72, *73*, 90, 110, 122, 124, 125, 135
Stowe 12, *25*, 25, *36*, 45, *58*, 59, 62, *64*, 65, 73, *89*, 90, 96, 102, 103, 109, 110, 136, 138
Stratfield Saye 26
Strawberry Hill 59
Stroud, Dorothy 5
Studley Royal *15*, 15, 53, *53*, 73, 99, 104, 115, *117*, *130*, 131
Sutton Place 137
Sweert, Emanuel 49
Switzer, Stephen 18, 50, 105, 108, 138, 140
Switzerland 102

Syon House 21, 37, *37*, 126
Taj Mahal 121
Talman, William 138
Tatton Park 47
Temple, Sir William 108
Texas 138
Thornton Manor 71
Tijou, Jean *33*, 34, 69, 106
Tisbury 62
Tivoli 52, 101, 103
Tradescant, John and John (father and son) 92
Trentham Park 22, 136
Troy House 18
Tudor House Museum, Southampton 72, *123*, 124
Turkey 69
Turner, Richard 85
Twickenham 81
Tyringham 138
United States of America 102
Valley Gardens, Windsor 126
Vanbrugh, Sir John 19, 25, 30, 62, 72, 81, 96, 102, 130, 140
Van Nost, John, the Elder 73, 114, 126
Vatican 19
Vauban, Sébastien Maréchal 76
Vauxhall Gardens 89, 90, 94, 123, 125
Versailles 15, 41, 52, 63, 111, 122, 129, 131
Vicenza 23, 88
Victoria and Albert Museum 98
Victoria Park, Bristol 76

Victoria Park, London 95
Vienna 19
Villa Aldobrandini 14, 28, 58, 112, 121
Villa Caprarola 30
Villa Cimbrone 19
Villa d'Este 14, 52, 132
Villa di Monte Solare *57*
Villa Giulia 80
Villa Lante 28, 30
Villa Medici 61
Villa Mondragone 58
Villandry *51*
Virginia 93
Virginia Water 48
Waddesdon Manor 14, *14*
Wakefield 107
Waldershare Park 19
Walpole, Horace 11, 27, 33, 34, 59, 108
Walton Bridge 72, 123
Wanstead 15, 138
Ward, Nathaniel 130
Wardour 91, 100
Warwick Castle 102
Wentworth Castle 23, 30, 59, 59, 110
Wentworth Woodhouse 26, 42, 98
Westbury Court 27, 34, 44, 46, 55, *56*, *63*, 96
West Dean 90, 139
Westonbirt Arboretum 12
Westonbirt House 5, 69, 74, 83, *91*, *120*
Weston Park 23, *117*, 136
West Wycombe Park *cover*, 18, 48, *49*, 75, 100, 110
Whately, Thomas 47, 99
White, Gilbert 62, 63, *133*

Whitton 98
Whitworth Hall *63*, 63
Wilhelmshöhe 11
Wilton House *24*, 25, 29, 133
Wimborne Minster 19, *41*
Wimpole Hall 18, 30, 136
Winchester Castle 76
Windsor Great Park 21, 126
Wise, Henry 98, 110, 138, 140
Wisley 68, 99
Witley Court 139
Woburn Abbey 10, 26, 41, *74*, 76, 85, 121, 125
Woburn Farm 47, 104
Woodbridge, Kenneth 5
Woollett, William 23
Worcester College, Oxford 36
Wotton 136
Wrest Park 16, *17*, 27, *32*, 34, 89, *89*, 138
Wright, Frank Lloyd 101
Wright, Stephen 23, 62
Wright, Thomas 16, 42, 66, 102, 104, 105, 140
Wrighte, William 105
Wroxton 108
Wyatt, James 23, 41
Wyatt, Samuel 54, 83, 128
Wyatville, Sir Jeffry 48, 115
Yorkshire Sculpture Park *106*, 107
Young, Arthur 104

THE GARDEN HISTORY SOCIETY

The Society was founded in 1965 to bring together those interested in garden history in its various aspects: garden and landscape design and their relation to architecture, art, literature, philosophy and society; plant introduction, propagation and taxonomy; estate and woodland planning and maintenance; and other related subjects. The Society, a statutory consultee, works to ensure the conservation of parks and gardens of historic interest and the adoption of historically valid methods of restoration and management. The journal of the society, *Garden History,* is published twice a year and members also receive a *Newsletter* three times a year. Visits and tours to parks and gardens of historic interest throughout Britain and overseas are arranged for members and there is an active Scottish group. Details of membership may be obtained from the Honorary Membership Secretary, 5 The Knoll, Hereford HR1 1RU, UK.